La Città del Sole

The City of the Sun

La Città del Sole:
Dialogo Poetico

The City of the Sun:
A Poetical Dialogue

Tommaso Campanella

TRANSLATED WITH
INTRODUCTION AND NOTES BY
DANIEL J. DONNO

UNIVERSITY
OF CALIFORNIA
PRESS

BERKELEY
LOS ANGELES
LONDON

Library of Congress Cataloging in Publication Data

Campanella, Tommaso, 1568–1639.
  La città del sole.

  (Biblioteca italiana)
  Translation of Civitas Solis.
  Translation based on the Italian text edited by
Luigi Firpo.
  Text in English and Italian; introd. and notes in
English.
  Bibliography: p.
  1. Utopias.   I. Donno, Daniel John, 1920–
II. Title.   III. Title: The City of the Sun.
HX811 1623.E980   335'.02   80-20133
ISBN 0-520-04034-1

University of California Press
Berkeley and Los Angeles, California

University of California Press, Ltd.
London, England

© 1981 by
The Regents of the University of California
Printed in the United States of America

1   2   3   4   5   6   7   8   9

Contents

Introduction

NOTWITHSTANDING the contradictions and inconsistencies, both real and imaginary, that scholars have noted in Tommaso Campanella's voluminous *oeuvre*, no one can doubt that for him life and thought were inseparable. Beginning in youth and continuing through a long, tormented life, he was sustained and guided by an unquenchable sense of mission that absorbed all his immense energies and left him indifferent to the gratifications, comforts, and rewards that men normally seek. He saw himself as the bearer of a message, the designer of a program for mankind involving nothing less than a thorough reform of virtually all human institutions, both secular and spiritual. To achieve this great mission he was willing to risk and endure imprisonment and torture time and time again, to work tirelessly under inhuman conditions for years on end. For him life had but one purpose, and an untimely death was to be shunned only because his mission would thereby be left unaccomplished. Even in his darkest hours he was not tempted by the solace of a martyr's death nor broken in spirit. He was only twenty-four when he entered the first of several prisons he would occupy during his life, and he was not completely free until he was sixty-one. He was a great survivor.

Even before he had come to write *The City of the Sun* he had experienced more than enough persecution to make its confident optimism seem implausible. Yet through the many more years of persecution that were to follow its composition his faith in the advent of a political, religious, and social renewal such as it envisioned rarely waivered. In such grim circumstances a more common man would have doubted whether so

sanguine a view of humanity's future was even remotely credible. Campanella never did. That he could sustain his hopes through so much suffering and at the same time pour out a stream of books ranging over almost every area of human knowledge is a fact that would strain belief without the evidence of the books themselves. Numerous as they are, they would be substantially more numerous if all that he wrote had survived.

Equally extraordinary is the fact that the two institutions chiefly responsible for his persecution—the Church of Rome and the Spanish monarchy—are presented in his writings as the most promising agents of his cherished reforms, as the instruments through which his philosophy would find its practical expression. Inevitably this has raised the question as to whether Campanella was being sincere. Certainly there have been formidable doubters, most notably Luigi Amabile. But it is now generally agreed that, though his pro-hispanism was probably tainted by self-interest—by his need to allay the suspicions of his tormentors and soften their hostility so as to win release from prison—his real views on religious and political matters were on the whole those he expressed openly again and again between 1594 and 1628. Indiscreet but fiercely tenacious, he was not one to play fast and loose with his beliefs even for his freedom.

On the contrary, disregarding all danger to himself, he had the boldness—not to say the temerity—to defend the unpopular opinions of others as vigorously as he defended his own. The case of Galileo, first in 1616 and then again in 1632, is an example. Certainly his spirited *Apologia pro Galileo* does not smack of opportunism, for it was written only a few months after the Holy Office had proscribed Copernicus' heliocentric theory and had forbidden the astronomer to teach it, as

Campanella well knew. The agonies and humiliations he had earlier suffered at the hands of that same Holy Office did not detain him from taking up the cause of a man whose views he did not share. As soon as the work was completed, moreover, he presented a copy to Cardinal Caetani, who had been given the task of expurgating Copernicus' *De revolutionibus*. Surely he recognized that opposition to such high authority was not the way to gain his freedom. At the time Campanella was passing through one of the grimmest periods of his imprisonment. He was confined—"buried," as he said in a letter to Galileo—in the windowless, damp dungeon of Castel S. Elmo, the worst of several Neapolitan fortresses in which he had already spent seventeen years (1599–1616) and was to spend ten more. Under the circumstances his *Apologia* was a remarkable feat of courage in the cause of learning.

The situation was to be very different in 1632. Having finally been released from his Neapolitan bondage in 1626, he was rearrested after a few scant weeks of liberty and transported to Rome, there to answer charges of heresy. Until 1629 he was confined to the precincts of the Holy Office and the monastery of S. Maria sopra Minerva. Then he was turned over to the custody of his Dominican superiors, and a period of real but still precarious freedom began. By then his many books had won him powerful supporters. Pope Urban VIII, on whose behalf he had employed his skill in astrology and magic, had assigned him a pension, and there were even rumors that he was to be invested with a cardinal's hat. After so many desperate years he had arrived at a position of influence, and everything seemed to augur well for the fulfillment of his great mission. It was a time to walk circumspectly and spare himself new difficulties. But Campanella could not be cautious.

In February 1632 Galileo published his great *Dialogue Concerning the Two Chief World Systems*, in which he reviewed the evidence for heliocentrism. Seven months after publication its sale was prohibited and, near the beginning of the following year, the author, old and in ill health, was summoned to the Holy Office and told that his work had been condemned. He was required to make a public abjuration of his views and was then sentenced to jail. This sentence, however, was immediately commuted to permanent house arrest. As in 1616, but now free and influential in the Roman Curia, Campanella again entered the lists on Galileo's behalf, offering his services as defender and risking his hard-won but still new-fledged prestige to obtain a reversal of the decision. It was a futile effort that only strengthened the hand of his enemies and cost him the pope's warm friendship. Campanella's letters to Galileo during this period show that he knew what risks he was taking. Yet he felt he was not doing enough. In a letter dated October 22, 1632, he apologized to his friend for his "cowardice born of prolonged sufferings and calumnies."

It was characteristic of him to underrate his courage. It was also characteristic of him not to let his own unhappy experiences determine his judgment of men and institutions—hence, in large part, his long adherence to Spain and his lifelong adherence to the Roman Church. He felt they had been divinely appointed to carry out the mission his messianic fervor envisioned for them. The proof of this was evident to him in history and in the stars.

Born the son of an illiterate cobbler in Stilo, Calabria, in 1568, Giovanni Domenico Campanella joined the Dominican order at fourteen, adopting the name Tommaso out of admiration for the great angelic doctor, the

chief luminary of the order. The step probably reflected a yearning for further education rather than an inclination to a clerical vocation, for in sixteenth-century Italy a youth with no private means had virtually no other way to pursue studies beyond the elementary level, and Campanella's love of learning was already very pronounced. Conspicuous for his large, powerful physique, endowed with enormous energy, insatiable curiosity, and a prodigious memory, he devoured books of every kind, the prohibited as well as the obligatory and the allowed. Very early, in fact, he began to display strong anti-Aristotelian tendencies that disturbed his superiors. Then in 1588 he was shown a copy of Bernardino Telesio's *De rerum natura* in the incomplete 1570 edition. Enthralled by it, he immediately set out to visit the octogenerian author, a fellow Calabrian and bishop of Cosenza, arriving only to find his body lying in state in the cathedral. After writing a Latin elegy, he affixed it to the bier and departed.

But Telesio's ideas were to leave a lasting mark on Campanella's thought, and his first significant work would be the *Philosophia sensibus demonstrata*, a defense of Telesio's anti-Aristotelianism, which he completed in seven months. Telesio had affirmed that all of nature is animated and endowed with varying degrees of sensation and that all that happens in nature results from the interaction of two opposing forces, heat and cold, the one emitted by the sun, the other by the earth. He urged that nature be studied at first hand, avoiding all presuppositions, and he advised that we seek to acquire knowledge by means of our senses, rather than through reason. "*Non ratione*," he declared, "*sed sensu*." These ideas pleased Campanella immensely since they tended strongly in the direction of his own thinking, but his enthusiastic espousal of them brought him into conflict with his superiors who preferred to trust in the en-

trenched authority of Aristotle for their philosophy and resented his habit of challenging all received opinion. Unable to brook intellectual restraints, Campanella left his isolated post in Altomonte without permission and made his way to Naples, where he took up residence in the convent of San Domenico Maggiore.

There, through the closing months of 1589 and for the next two years, he was active in several learned circles where he became acquainted with Giambattista Della Porta, the noted dramatist and polymath, who apparently encouraged him to pursue his already lively interest in magic and the other occult sciences. He saw his *Philosophia sensibus demonstrata* through the press and wrote *De investigatione rerum* and *De sensu rerum* (both of which would soon be seized from him by agents of the Holy Office). But in Naples too his study of magic, combined with his outspoken anti-Aristotelianism, set him at odds with some of his fellow Dominicans. Charges of a rather indeterminate nature were brought against him (among them, a charge that he kept a familiar devil, to whom he owed his great learning, lodged beneath one of his fingernails), and the grim pattern of events that he was to experience again and again began to unfold. He was arrested, imprisoned briefly in San Domenico, and then tried. On this occasion, as on graver ones later, the real verdict of his judges is unknown. All we know is that in August 1592 he was ordered to abandon his Telesian views, to leave Naples within a week, and to return to Altomonte. Disregarding these orders, he journeyed to Florence instead, whence had come some vague promise of a professorial chair at one of the Tuscan universities. The expectation proved illusory, however, and he soon continued on to Padua where he became acquainted with Galileo and Paolo Sarpi. There he enjoyed almost a year of complete freedom during which he flung himself into new

projects. He wrote the *Apologia pro Telesio* and the *Rhetorica nova* along with other works which introduced the religio-political thesis he was to develop at great length under far less happy circumstances.

Having got possession of all his manuscripts by theft more than a year before, the Holy Office stepped in again in 1594, arresting him upon a variety of charges, one of them being that he had discussed questions of faith with a lapsed Jewish *converso*. During the investigation that followed, torture was twice applied to force a confession from him. When this failed, he was remanded to prison for the remainder of the year, and then, without permission obtained from the civil authorities to extradite him, he was clandestinely transported to Rome, where his incarceration continued until the next year. Giordano Bruno, with whose ideas Campanella's have often been associated (though the two probably never met), had preceded him to the same prison of the Inquisition several years before and would leave it only to walk to the stake in 1600. During this period Campanella continued to write, defending his philosophy, seeking character references, pleading for support or protection wherever he might find it. But nothing helped. In May 1595, after again being tortured, he was condemned upon grave suspicion of heresy and ordered to make a humiliating public recantation of his doctrines. This time he yielded, just as Galileo was to do thirty-eight years later. Then, as part of his sentence, he took up obligatory residence in the monastery of S. Sabina on the Aventine.

There he wrote a work on physics, another on poetics, and a *Dialogue against Lutherans, Calvinists and Other Heretics*. This relatively mild detention might have lasted for many years, but mischance intervened. On March 5, 1597, a Calabrian bandit about to be hanged in Naples divulged "secret" information making Campa-

nella out a heretic, and once again the prison doors of the Inquisition opened for him. Months of apparent indecision on the part of the authorities ensued before he was released and again ordered to return to Calabria. Reluctantly, he obeyed. After a somewhat prolonged stopover in Naples, he was back in the monastery of S. Maria de Gesú in his native Stilo by the fall of 1598. He was then barely thirty years old.

Undaunted by his terrible experiences as a prisoner in Naples, Padua, and Rome, still full of wild hopes and irrepressible energy, he now embarked upon the most dangerous and ultimately the most ruinous enterprise of his life. He abandoned his passive role as thinker to become a man of action, publicly lashing out at both the Church and the Spanish authorities, apparently with the design of making himself the direct agent of the religious, political, and social renewal he wished to see implemented. Since there is scarcely any evidence that he had changed his mind at this date about the roles he had announced for the Church and Spain, it is difficult to explain why he now attacked them. It may be that he planned to establish a model commonwealth which they were then to imitate on a worldwide scale, or it may be that he was simply driven to action by what he had deduced from old prophecies, recent natural disasters, and astral configurations, all portending that the year 1600 would witness great upheavals and sweeping changes. But we really do not know, since much of the information about this crucial episode derives from the statements of men testifying under torture or threats of torture and death. It is certain in any case that on September 6, 1599, Campanella was arrested along with some 150 others and transported to Naples in chains.

Under the brutal, unconcealed tyranny of Spain, often operating in league with the ubiquitous Inquisition, the provinces of southern Italy had been reduced

to such pitiful straits that the danger of sudden popular uprisings was ever present. There had been several in that century. Secular and ecclesiastical authorities were widely regarded as mere exploiters of the native population. Extreme poverty, high unemployment, and every kind of repression had driven a large number of the able-bodied to take up banditry and organized brigandage as regular vocations, the only ones promising them subsistence. Among these elements, and among the many who sympathized with them, the emergence of any leader who could give them some promise of success was all the tinder needed to start a conflagration.

That a revolt against both the Church establishment and the government had been planned during the summer of 1599 is beyond doubt, and that Campanella was somehow prominently involved from the beginning is scarcely less certain. Such debate as there is concerns the precise nature of his involvement, and most authorities (Amabile, Amerio, Bobbio, and Firpo among them) assign him a major role, if not indeed the leading one, for there is considerable agreement between Campanella's published views and the testimony of hostile witnesses who, being illiterate, could have learned them only from Campanella's own lips. The aims of the rising, it would appear, were to drive out the Spanish powers, subdue the ecclesiastical authorities, and reorder Calabria as a theocratic, communistic state along lines that are developed in *The City of the Sun*. At the appropriate moment a Turkish fleet was to materialize off the coast to aid the rebels. Though Campanella even under torture vehemently denied that he was guilty of either heresy or sedition, he did confess to having preached that the turn of the century would be marked by great political changes. His co-conspirators went beyond this, saying that he had spoken of floods, earthquakes, stellar conjunctions, and other evidence signaling the

imminence of a new age in which all men would enjoy their "natural freedom." Inspired by Campanella, perhaps other friars had made similar messianic pronouncements. But many who joined the conspiracy doubtless had less lofty motivations, seeing no more in it than an opportunity to pillage, steal, and settle old scores.

The existence of the plot became known to the authorities well before the revolt could get underway. After a brief flight, Campanella was put into the hands of his pursuers by a friend whom his father had once rescued from death. Shortly later he was transported to Naples with a motley retinue of true and suspected allies, and then the long dark period of his life began.

A series of inconclusive trials interrupted by jurisdictional disputes between the secular and ecclesiastical authorities followed. In none of these was Campanella actually pronounced guilty of either heresy or sedition. But he continued to be regarded as too dangerous a man to let go, and late in 1602, more than two years after his capture, the Inquisition sentenced him to life imprisonment without hope of reprieve. The civil trial for sedition meanwhile went on and, in fact, was never brought to a formal conclusion. Harsh as the sentence was, Campanella had expected nothing less than the death sentence, and he had already been long engaged in a plan to thwart its ever being carried out. For he knew that, though torture had failed to extract a full confession from him, he had nevertheless been forced to reveal a good deal of incriminating evidence. He also knew, however, that under canon law an insane man's repentance was invalid and that the execution of such a man would therefore consign him to eternal damnation. This no mortal judge could take it upon himself to do.

On Easter Sunday, 1601, therefore, he set fire to the

pallet in his cell and began to feign insanity, a deception he continued for the next fourteen months. Meanwhile, his far from credulous jailers spied on him night and day and twice tested him under torture without ever swaying him from his course. It is to his cleverness in devising such a scheme and to his extraordinary fortitude in carrying it through that he owed his life. The second of the two tests under torture was the most barbarous ordeal he ever underwent. For more than thirty-six hours without pause he was subjected to *la veglia* (the wake). His arms were twisted behind him and bound at the wrists by a rope that at the same time allowed him to hold himself suspended a few inches above a seat fitted with sharp wooden spikes. When the pain in his arms and shoulders became unbearable, he was compelled to seek relief by lowering himself on the spikes, which would then tear into his flesh. His courage in not betraying himself to his tormentors through this terrible ordeal won for him what was tantamount to a certificate of insanity, and thereafter he was no longer in danger of execution.

Until 1604 he was held in Castel Nuovo, where conditions were relatively tolerable. Then, after an attempted escape, he was transferred to the damp underground dungeon of Castel S. Elmo, where, chained hand and foot, he would remain for the next four years. As he was to say more than once, that dungeon was his Caucasus, where, like the bound Prometheus, he was restrained from accomplishing his mission to mankind. Astonishingly, despite the chains and the darkness, he wrote some of his most moving lyrics there as well as the *Monarchia del messia* and the *Atheismus triumphatus*, sometimes using blank sheets of paper that his guards, having been bribed, periodically slipped into his breviary. It is said that he underwent a conversion from which he emerged more deeply convinced of his mes-

sianic mission and more accepting of his suffering. In 1608 he was released from the dungeon and restored to better quarters where he could write with less difficulty and even receive visitors. This happier situation lasted until 1614 when, apparently as a result of his indirect contact with the outside world, old suspicions were rekindled and he was returned to his shackles in S. Elmo for four more wretched years. Still, his writing never ceased. *Quod reminiscentur*, much of the *Theologia*, the *Apologia pro Galileo*, along with works on rhetoric, poetics, medicine, dialectics, and astrology, date from this period—amazing achievements, since for lengthy periods Campanella was without books and had to trust to his memory for facts and citations.

In 1618 he was once again released from his dungeon and returned to fairly humane confinement in Castel Nuovo. There he devoted most of his energy to the completion of works already underway, to revising and translating them from Latin to Italian and vice versa. There too he became even more active in his relentless endeavor to regain his freedom, a goal he never despaired of achieving and toward which he had begun to work even while awaiting sentence. Now, being better known, he could appeal to a larger number of individuals to intercede for him. Letter after letter went out to influential sympathizers, learned acquaintances, powerful churchmen, and monarchs, pleading his case and promising to accomplish great things, not only in the world of learning but also in technology and even in finance once he was at liberty.

In May 1626 all these efforts seemed to come to fruition. He was released and permitted to return to the same Neapolitan monastery where thirty-five years earlier he had had his first taste of prison life. But this was merely a false dawn. Only a few weeks later he was arrested again by orders of the papal nuncio and trans-

ported to Rome, chained and in disguise, for his release had come through the secular authorities and was deeply resented by the Inquisition. There he was confined in the Holy Office for three more years while he fought fiercely and on the whole successfully to clear his books from charges of doctrinal errors. Not until 1629 did he begin that short decade of freedom that would end with his death at the age of seventy-one, after having spent nearly half his entire life in confinement.

Half of that short decade of freedom was passed in Rome. It was in this period that he enjoyed and then lost the favor of Pope Urban VIII, who, fancying himself a poet, was flattered by an elaborate commentary Campanella provided for his youthful verses. For a while he was listened to in the Curia, but his sudden change of fortune inevitably aroused jealousy, and his efforts to establish a missionary college and get his books approved for publication (many of them having already appeared in Germany) were successfully obstructed. So too were his efforts, undertaken against the pope's own wishes, to get Galileo's great dialogue a fair hearing in 1632. The event that ended his Roman sojourn, however, came two years later when one of his former disciples was found to be involved in a conspiracy directed against the Spanish viceroy in Naples. Campanella was immediately suspected of complicity, and the Spanish authorities put strong pressure on the pope to obtain his extradition to Naples. Unwilling to appear weak or submissive, though his enthusiasm for Campanella had now cooled, the pope joined with the French ambassador in a scheme to get him safely out of the way. Accordingly, once again assuming a disguise, Campanella slipped quietly out of the Holy City and made his way to France.

Welcomed to Paris by both Louis XIII and Richelieu—doubtless in part because he had some years be-

fore abandoned his advocacy of Spanish supremacy—
he spent his last years there in relative peace, busily
preparing his books for the press while devoting his
considerable polemical talents to the conversion of
Protestants, with remarkable success if the testimony of
his letters is to be trusted. Early in 1639, foreseeing his
imminent death in the stars, he sought to nullify their
malefic influence by resorting to propitiatory rites he
had found apparently efficacious in 1626 when he had
applied them on behalf of Urban VIII in similar circum-
stances; but he died on May 21 of that year in the Do-
minican monastery in Rue St. Honoré.

In all, Campanella is believed to have written more
than a hundred books, some of which were taken from
him and never returned, others simply lost. Those that
have survived form a very large corpus. Among these,
The City of the Sun is one of the shortest, but ever since
its initial publication in 1623 it has remained the best
known, the only one that has enjoyed a measure of pop-
ular favor. Some students of Campanella's writings do
not attach great importance to it within the whole con-
text of his thought, especially when it is set against
works of vastly greater complexity and breadth like the
Theologia. Others—certainly the majority—have
found in it the germ of virtually all his major ideas. If we
may judge by the author's own frequent references to it,
we must conclude that he had a high regard for it
throughout his life. As late as 1637 we find him writing
to Richelieu to express the hope that the Cardinal would
build the *Civitas solis* he had designed.

Campanella wrote *The City of the Sun* in Castel
Nuovo in 1602, the same year he was sentenced to life
imprisonment and only three years after the aborted
Calabrian uprising. It has often been regarded as an
idealized description of the society he had hoped would

emerge from that brash and disastrous undertaking. But we know that even by this date he had abandoned any expectation of bringing about a fundamental reordering of society through violence while he continued passionately to believe in the need for such a reordering. Before vital institutions could be radically improved, he now recognized, men's hearts and minds would have to be changed. We note that the Solarians, as the citizens of his utopia are called, do not engage in warfare to impose their way of life upon their very different neighboring states. They live in a "philosophic community" and are governed according to reason and the law of nature by a philosopher who is at once both prince and priest. Here we have a glimpse of the theocracy Campanella hoped would one day universally obtain. To him, indeed, this was more than a hope. It was a certainty, and his sacred duty was to hasten the day of its coming. Up to the early 1630s he believed that Providence had appointed the Spanish monarchy to be the secular instrument through which a worldwide Catholic hegemony would be established. To him, Spain's vast possessions around the globe were a sign of divine favor. In his last years, however, recognizing the corruptness and fragility of that far-flung empire, he came to believe that this role had passed to France. But the universal Roman Church Campanella envisaged was to be very different from that of his own day. It would be stripped of doctrinal inessentials, cleansed of ecclesiastical abuses, and broadened sufficiently to win over the adherents of other sects without compromising its fundamental truths. The pontiff would be both spiritual and secular master of this all-encompassing empire. In fact, spiritual and secular functions would no longer be sharply distinguishable, for, as Campanella observed in a letter to Pope Paul V, canon law would suffice for all purposes, and civil law could be disposed of.

15

In Campanella's view, religion is a universal impulse, the innate possession off all beings; and since all things are endowed with sense, all things worship their Creator in diverse degrees and derive their understanding of Him through their study of His creation. It follows, therefore, that science—what is learned from nature—cannot be in conflict with true theology. On the contrary, the latter must be deduced from the former. It also follows that scripture and nature are in harmony, revealing the same truths in different ways. Being rational, the Solarians of course worship God, addressing Him through His creation; and they honor the sun as His sensible image. They have heard of Christ, but are not yet "in possession of revelation." In this respect, as in others, they resemble Thomas More's Utopians, who, though ignorant of Christ until Raphael Hythloday's arrival among them, had nevertheless deduced a decidedly Christian conception of the deity through reason alone. Indeed, the Solarians have proceeded far enough to worhip God in the Trinity, though they cannot yet "distinguish and name the three persons." When at some future date they become fully converted to Christianity, they will learn that it "adds nothing but the sacraments to the law of nature and is entirely congruent with it." Hence the inevitable conclusion that "Christianity is the true law and . . . once its abuses have been corrected, it will become mistress of the world." Given this conception of Christianity, it is easy to understand why Campanella has been called a Deist or has been said to incline toward Deism. His lifelong ecumenical fervor, in any case, is very much in harmony with the religious spirit of our own day.

Hierarchical in structure but egalitarian in spirit, Campanella's utopia is a powerful state with interests identical to those of its citizens. All positions of authority are won and held by merit alone, every citizen con-

tributes his physical labor in some measure to the performance of essential tasks, and all adults of both sexes are subject to military service when it is needed. Work is not an end in itself; it is simply the means by which necessary and only necessary goods and services are provided and by which the individual fulfills himself by applying his particular talents. Surplus production, even when it is exportable, is generally avoided, and no one need work beyond the four hours each day that experience has proved sufficient for all requirements. All necessary tasks, no matter how lowly, have their inherent dignity, and the skillful performance of them is honorable. Women enjoy equal status with men, though differences in strength, temperament, and inclination make them more suited to some tasks—the less strenuous, for example—than to others. But they receive the same education as men, being trained in both the mechanical and the speculative arts. They have equal voice in council and may hold any position for which they are qualified.

Like More's, Campanella's utopia is communistic and antimaterialistic. The unitary family and private ownership of property are both prohibited because these institutions are regarded as the foundations of egoism, setting citizens in competition with one another against their common interests and against the collective interests of the state. The procreation and rearing of offspring are therefore concerns of the commonwealth. Adults are free to gratify their normal sexual impulses so long as there is no danger of accidental pregnancy. When pregnancy is desired by the state, designated officials are charged with selecting the couples to be mated in accordance with recognized eugenic principles. Thus birth control is employed not so much to limit the population as to improve its physical and mental capacities.

Education is given the greatest attention. It is free,

17

compulsory, and continous. Here Campanella antici-
pates some of those cherished ideas his admirer Come-
nius was to work hard to promote later in the same cen-
tury. Much of the available space in *The City of the Sun*,
for example, is reserved for permanent exhibits of all
kinds: astronomical, geographical, zoological, botani-
cal, mineralogical, mechanical, and so on. In these, ac-
tual specimens are displayed whenever possible so that
students may be in contact with real things, which are
the best teachers, rather than with mere pictures and
models. Since these exhibits are on view on all save the
outer wall of the seven-walled city, its streets are verita-
ble classrooms and museums. Given this remarkable
emphasis on education, it is not surprising that learning
proceeds rapidly on all levels. Only two days, for ex-
ample, are needed to learn any one of the mechanical
arts. No wonder, then, that the Solarians know how to
fly! They also appear to have made great strides in medi-
cine, hygiene, and dietetics, thanks to the importance—
unusual in Campanella's day—they attribute to them.
Indeed, it is striking that the Solarians, though they es-
tablished their utopia as a philosophic community, de-
vote a good deal less attention to philosophic specula-
tion than to purely practical concerns. Their chief aim,
it seems, is to live comfortably in peace and pursue
knowledge, not as an end in itself, but as the means to
reduce drudgery and pain and to enhance the pleasant-
ness of life. Hence the heavy stress on science and tech-
nology and the relatively scant attention given to tran-
scendent and supernatural things.

Oddly, but not inexplicably, much that seems for-
ward-looking or even modern in *The City of the Sun*
goes hand in hand with attitudes that were already out
of fashion when it was written. A fondness for monasti-
cism is an example. Too independent and restless to
abide a monastery himself, Campanella nevertheless re-

tained a lifelong admiration for the communal life of the cloister and believed that, properly reformed, it could provide a model for all society. Perhaps equally odd to a modern reader is his enduring commitment to astrology, which he found entirely compatible with his commitment to reason and to the law of nature. It should appear less odd, however, when it is recalled that scientists of the stature of Johannes Kepler and Tycho Brahe saw nothing incongruous between their astronomical investigations and their casting of horoscopes and that such forerunners of modern thought as Bruno, Bacon, and Leibnitz were far from spurning the "occult sciences." Throughout the Renaissance these "sciences" attracted the favorable attention of some of the keenest minds, for as the fixed and static medieval view of man crumbled, it seemed that new powers and new mysteries were being discovered. They had somehow to be controlled, and the need itself encouraged the belief that the means to do so, whether visible or invisible, were at hand. Campanella's confidence in astrology therefore reflects some of the deepest concerns of his age.

Of most interest to the modern reader, perhaps, is Campanella's rare awareness of the deep-rooted moral confusion of his age, its gross distortion of human values, its waste of human life, its crass injustice, and its readiness to accept such conditions as inevitable. In sketching out his utopia, he offered some bold and novel remedies embodying a vision of man's earthly destiny that can still provoke and enlighten.

The Text of *The City of the Sun*

The original version of *The City of the Sun*, written in Italian in 1602, did not appear in print until the first years of this century. For a period it circulated in manuscript, and some fifteen copies have been located. Far better known was a Latin translation Campanella com-

pleted in 1613 at the request of a German admirer, Tobia
Adami, who felt that in that form it would attract a
larger audience. Entitled *Civitas solis*, this version was
published in Frankfurt in 1623. Under Campanella's
own supervision it was reprinted in Paris in 1637, form-
ing a small part of his voluminous *Philosophia realis*.
Thereafter, it seems, the Italian original was completely
forgotten, for in 1836, when G. B. Passerini wanted his
fellow Italians to learn about Campanella's communis-
tic state, he was obliged to make his own translation
using the Paris edition, which also served as the source
for translations into other languages, including En-
glish. Thus for nearly three centuries the work was
known only in Latin or in less than adequate transla-
tions deriving from it.

In this century scholars have returned to the original
text because it more accurately expresses Campanella's
thinking. A number of Italian editions have appeared,
but not until 1941, when Norberto Bobbio's version
came from the press, did a truly critical text become
available. Bobbio based his edition upon a careful ex-
amination of ten of the eleven manuscripts then known,
the British Museum copy being unavailable to him
owing to the war. Luigi Firpo later located four addi-
tional manuscripts that provided the basis for a few not
especially notable departures from Bobbio's text. These
he introduced into his own 1949 edition that appeared in
Scritti scelti di Giordano Bruno e Tommaso Campanella,
and it is this text that I have used for the present transla-
tion. It is the only complete and unexpurgated version
in English. It is also the only one based on Campanella's
Italian original. Thomas W. Halliday's 1885 version,
frequently reprinted, omits or bowdlerizes just about
everything the author has to say about eugenics and
sexual matters. There are also notable omissions in
W. J. Gilstrap's version (published in G. Negley and

J. Max Patrick, *The Quest for Utopia* [New York, 1952]). These chiefly concern Campanella's astrology —certainly the most intractable material in the text, at least for a translator—and his views on warfare.

In subtitling his work *A Poetical Dialogue* Campanella meant only to call attention to its fictional character without intending to claim specifically literary merits for it. Obviously, he wrote in some haste and was often too impatient to pause for the precise word, eliminate minor inconsistencies, revise, and polish. He was also generally averse to adornment and elaboration, often inserting a hurried *etc.* where fleshing out his meaning in some detail, though not vital, would have been helpful. Frequently, the result is a sense of sketchiness. Yet he is rarely unclear.

In the present translation I have tried to avoid misrepresenting his plain, spare style, and have sought primarily for accuracy and clarity. The notes for the most part are intended to elucidate the text as economically as possible. Only in a few instances have I felt it necessary to refer to some one of his many, but often uncertain, sources. With the astrological material, however, a special problem arises: Campanella all too obviously assumes that his readers are at home with the concepts and terms he employs. Those who are not may find some comfort in the generally ampler notes I have provided for this material, but they are cautioned that the annotator himself can lay no claim to expertise in that abstruse and cloudy science.

In preparing this short work I have profited from the labors of numerous *campanellisti*, chiefly those already named, but my greatest debt, clearly, is to Luigi Firpo.

TEXT AND TRANSLATION

F. Thomæ Campanellæ
Appendix Politicæ
Civitas Solis
Idea Reipvblicæ Philosophicæ

Brother Thomas Campanella's
Appendix to the *Politics*
The City of the Sun
The Idea of a Philosophic Republic

La Città del Sole

di Fra Tommaso Campanella

DIALOGO POETICO

INTERLOCUTORI

Ospitalario e Genovese nochiero del Colombo

OSPITALARIO. Dimmi, di grazia, tutto quello che t'avvenne in questa navigazione.

GENOVESE. Già t'ho detto come girai il mondo tutto, e poi come arrivai alla Taprobana e fui forzato metter in terra, e poi, fuggendo la furia di terrazzani, mi rinselvai, e uscii in un gran piano proprio sotto l'equinoziale.

OSPITALARIO. Qui che t'occorse?

GENOVESE. Subito incontrai un gran squadrone d'uomini e donne armate, e molti di loro intendevano la lingua mia, li quali mi condussero alla Città del Sole.

OSPITALARIO. Di' come è fatta questa città e come si governa.

GENOVESE. Sorge nell'ampia campagna un colle, sopra il quale sta la maggior parte della città; ma arrivano i suoi giri molto spazio fuor delle radici del monte, il quale è tanto, che la città fa due miglia di diametro e più, e viene ad essere sette miglia di circolo; ma, per la levatura, più abitazioni ha, che si fosse in piano.

È la città distinta in sette gironi grandissimi, nominati dalli sette pianeti, e s'entra dall'uno all'altro per quattro strade e per quattro porte, alli quattro angoli del mondo spettanti; ma sta in modo che, se fosse espugnato il

The City of the Sun

by Brother Tommaso Campanella

A POETICAL DIALOGUE

INTERLOCUTORS

A Knight Hospitaler[1] and a Genoese, one of Columbus'
sailors

HOSPITALER. Tell me, please, all that happened to you on this voyage.

GENOESE. I have already told you how I sailed around the world and came to Taprobana, where I was forced to put ashore, how I hid in a forest to escape the fury of the natives, and how I came out onto a great plain just below the equator.[2]

HOSPITALER. What happened to you there?

GENOESE. I soon came upon a large company of armed men and women, and many of them understood my language. They led me to the City of the Sun.[3]

HOSPITALER. Tell me, what is that city like, and how is it ruled?

GENOESE. Rising from a broad plain, there is a hill upon which the greater part of the city is situated, but its circling walls extend far beyond its base, so that the entire city is two miles and more in diameter and has a circumference of seven miles; but because it is on a rise, it contains more habitations than it would if it were on a plain.[4]

The city is divided into seven large circuits, named after the seven planets. Passage from one to the other is provided by four avenues and four gates facing the four points of the compass. It is constructed in such a way that if the first circuit were taken by assault, more effort

27

primo girone, bisogna più travaglio al secondo e poi più; talchè sette fiate bisogna espugnarla per vincerla. Ma io son di parere, che neanche il primo si può, tanto è grosso e terrapieno, e ha valguardi, torrioni, artelleria e fossati di fuora.

Entrati dunque per la porta Tramontana, di ferro coperta, fatta che s'alza e cala con bello ingegno, si vede un piano di cinquanta passi tra la muraglia prima e l'altra. Appresso stanno palazzi tutti uniti per giro col muro, che puoi dir che tutti siano uno; e di sopra han li rivellini sopra a colonne, come chiostri di frati, e di sotto non vi è introito, se non dalla parte concava delli palazzi. Poi son le stanze belle con le finestre al convesso el al concavo, e son distinte con picciole mura tra loro. Solo il muro convesso è grosso otto palmi, il concavo tre, li mezzani uno o poco più.

Appresso poi s'arriva al secondo piano, ch'è dui passi o tre manco, e si vedono le seconde mura con li rivellini in fuora e passeggiatòri; e dalla parte dentro, l'altro muro, che serra i palazzi in mezzo, ha il chiostro con le colonne di sotto, e di sopra belle pitture.

E così s'arriva fin al supremo e sempre per piani. Solo quando s'entran le porte, che son doppie per le mura interiori ed esteriori, si ascende per gradi tali, che non si conosce, perchè vanno obliquamente, e son d'altura quasi insensibile distinte le scale.

Nella summità del monte vi è un gran piano e un gran tempio in mezzo, di stupendo artifizio.

OSPITALARIO. Di', di' mo, per vita tua.

would be required to take the second, likewise again the third, and so forth, so that seven assaults would be needed to conquer it all. But in my opinion not even the first assault would be successful, so thick is the wall, which, moreover, is guarded by ramparts, towers, artillery, and surrounding moats.

Entering by the northern gate, which is plated with iron and is raised and lowered by an ingenious device, you see a level area, some fifty paces wide, dividing the first circuit from the next. Girding the second wall there is a row of buildings which connect with it in such a way that you may say they are all one. Above them, there are ravelins[5] raised on columns like friars' cloisters. These can only be entered on the concave side of the buildings. Then there are fine rooms separated from one another by thin walls and supplied with windows both on the convex and concave sides. The convex wall is over six feet thick, the concave about two and a half, and the party walls about one.

Beyond, you come to the second level area, two or three paces narrower than the first. From here you can see the second circuit with its ravelins and passageways. The inner side of this one has the columned cloister below and beautiful paintings on the surface above.

Continuing in this manner, you finally come to the innermost circuit, always proceeding across level spaces. Only when you arrive at the circuit gates, which are double—there being one for the exterior side and another for the interior—do you ascend from one level to the next by way of slanting steps of scarcely noticeable height.

At the summit of the hill there is a spacious plain in the center of which rises an enormous temple of astonishing design.

HOSPITALER. Tell me more, I beg you, tell me more.

29

GENOVESE. Il tempio è tondo perfettamente, e non ha muraglia che lo circonda; ma sta situato sopra colonne grosse e belle assai. La cupola grande ha in mezzo una cupoletta con uno spiraglio, che pende sopra l'altare, ch'è un solo e sta nel mezzo del tempio. Girano le colonne trecento passi e più, e fuor delle colonne della cupola vi sono per otto passi li chiostri con mura poco elevate sopra le sedie, che stan d'intorno al concavo dell'esterior muro, benchè in tutte le colonne interiori, che senza muro fraposto tengono il tempio insieme, non manchino sedili portatili assai.

Sopra l'altare non vi è altro ch'un mappamondo assai grande, dove tutto il cielo è dipinto, e un altro dove è la terra. Poi sul cielo della cupola vi stanno tutte le stelle maggiori del cielo, notate coi nomi loro e virtù, c'hanno sopra le cose terrene, con tre versi per una; ci son i poli e i circoli signati non del tutto, perchè manca il muro a basso, ma si vedono finiti in corrispondenza alli globbi dell'altare. Vi sono sempre accese sette lampade nominate dalli sette pianeti.

Sopra il tempio vi stanno alcune celle nella cupoletta attorno, e molte altre grandi sopra li chiostri, e qui abitano li religiosi, che son da quaranta, ecc.

Vi è sopra la cupola una banderola per mostrare i venti, e ne signano trentasei; e sanno quando spira ogni vento che stagione porta. E qui sta anco un libro in lettere d'oro di cose importantissime.

OSPITALARIO. Per tua fè, dimmi tutto il modo del governo, chè qui t'aspettavo.

GENOVESE. È un principe sacerdote tra loro, che s'appella Sole, e in lingua nostra si dice Metafisico: questo è

GENOESE. The temple is perfectly circular and has no enclosing walls. It rests on large, well-proportioned columns. The large dome has a cupola at its center with an aperture directly above the single altar in the middle of the temple. The columns are arranged in a circle having a circumference of three hundred paces or more. Eight paces beyond them are cloisters with walls scarcely rising above the benches which are arranged along the concave exterior wall. Among the interior columns, which support the temple with no interposing walls, there are a large number of portable chairs.

Nothing rests on the altar but a huge celestial globe, upon which all the heavens are described, with a terrestrial globe beside it. On the vault of the dome overhead appear all the larger stars with their names and the influences they each have upon earthly things set down in three verses. The poles and circles are indicated,[6] but not entirely since there is no wall below. Instead they are completed on the globes resting on the altar below. Seven lamps, each named for one of the seven planets, are always kept burning.

Around the cupola at the top of the temple there are cells, and there are many other larger ones above the cloisters. These are inhabited by the clergy, who are forty in number.

Rising above the cupola there is a pennon to indicate the various winds, these being thirty-six in all, and the weather that accompanies each of these is known. Here too there is a book in which matters of the utmost importance are inscribed in letters of gold.

HOSPITALER. In good faith, tell me the manner of government you found among these people.

GENOESE. They have a Prince Prelate among them whom they call Sun, but in our language he would be called Metaphysician.[7] He is both their spiritual and

capo di tutti in spirituale e temporale, e tutti li negozi in lui si terminano.

Ha tre prìncipi collaterali: Pon, Sin, Mor, che vuol dir: Potestà, Sapienza e Amore.

Il Potestà ha cura delle guerre e delle paci e dell'arte militare; è supremo nella guerra, ma non sopra Sole; ha cura dell'offiziali, guerrieri, soldati, munizioni, fortificazioni ed espugnazioni.

Il Sapienza ha cura di tutte le scienze e delli dottori e magistrati dell'arti liberali e meccaniche, e tiene sotto di sè tanti offiziali quante son le scienze: ci è l'Astrologo, il Cosmografo, il Geometra, il Loico, il Rettorico, il Grammatico, il Medico, il Fisico, il Politico, il Morale; e tiene un libro solo, dove stan tutte le scienze, che fa leggere a tutto il popolo ad usanza di Pitagorici. E questo ha fatto pingere in tutte le muraglie, su li rivellini, dentro e di fuori, tutte le scienze.

Nelle mura del tempio esteriori e nelle cortine, che si calano quando si predica per non perdersi la voce, vi sta ogni stella ordinatamente con tre versi per una.

Nel dentro del primo girone tutte le figure matematiche, più che ne scrisse Euclide e Archimede, con la lor proposizione significante. Nel di fuore vi è la carta della terra tutta, e poi le tavole d'ogni provinzia con li riti e costumi e leggi loro, e con l'alfabeti ordinati sopra il loro alfabeto.

Nel dentro del secondo girone vi son tutte le pietre preziose e non preziose, e minerali, e metalli veri e pinti, con le dichiarazioni di due versi per uno. Nel di fuore vi son tutte sorti di laghi, mari e fiumi, vini e ogli e altri

their temporal chief, and all decisions terminate with him.

There are also three collateral princes: Pon, Sin, and Mor, that is to say Power, Wisdom, and Love.[8]

Power has charge of war and peace and of military affairs. He is supreme in war, but not above Sun. He has charge over officers, warriors, soldiers, munitions, fortifications, and sieges.

Wisdom has charge of all the sciences and of all the doctors and masters of the liberal and mechanical arts. Below him there are as many officers as there are sciences. There is an Astrologer, a Cosmographer, a Geometer, a Logician, a Rhetorician, a Grammarian, a Physician, a Physical Scientist,[9] a Politician, and a Moralist. Wisdom has but one book in which all the sciences are treated and which is taught to all the people after the manner of the Pythagoreans.[10] He has had all of the sciences pictured on all of the walls and on the ravelins, both inside and out.[11]

On the exterior walls of the temple, on the curtains which are let down when there is preaching so that it may be heard, all the stars are drawn in order, with three descriptive verses assigned to each one.

On the inner wall of the first circuit,[12] all the mathematical figures—more than Euclid or Archimedes speaks of—are shown in their significant propositions. On the outer wall there is a map of the entire world with charts for each country setting forth their rites, customs, and laws; and the alphabet of each is inscribed above the native one.

On the inner wall of the second circuit there are both samples and pictures of all minerals, metals, and stones, both precious and nonprecious, with two descriptive verses for each one. On the outer wall all kinds of lakes, seas, rivers, wines, oils, and other liquids are shown with their sources of origin, their powers, and their

liquori, e loro virtù e origini e qualità; e ci son le caraffe piene di diversi liquori di cento e trecento anni, con li quali sanano tutte l'infirmità quasi.

Nel dentro del terzo vi son tutte le sorti di erbe e arbori del mondo pinte, e pur in teste di terra sopra il rivellino, e le dichiarazioni dove prima si ritrovâro, e le virtù loro, e le simiglianze c'hanno con le stelle e con li metalli e con le membra umane, e l'uso loro in medicina. Nel di fuora tutte maniere di pesci di fiumi, lachi e mari, e le virtù loro, e 'l modo di vivere, di generarsi e allevarsi, e a che serveno, e le somiglianze c'hanno con le cose celesti e terrestri e dell'arte e della natura; sì che mi stupii, quando trovai pesce vescovo e catena e chiodo e stella, appunto come son queste cose tra noi. Ci sono ancini, rizzi, spondoli e tutto quanto è degno di sapere con mirabil arte di pittura e di scrittura che dichiara.

Nel quarto, dentro vi son tutte sorti di uccelli pinti e lor qualità, grandezze e costumi, e la fenice è verissima appresso loro. Nel di fuora stanno tutte sorti di animali reptili, serpi, draghi, vermini, e l'insetti, mosche, tafani ecc., con le loro condizioni, veneni e virtuti; e son più che non pensamo.

Nel quinto, dentro vi son l'animali perfetti terrestri di tante sorti che è stupore. Non sappiamo noi la millesima parte, e però, sendo grandi di corpo, l'han pinti ancora nel di fuori rivellino; e quante maniere di cavalli solamente! oh, belle figure dichiarate dottamente!

Nel sesto, dentro vi sono tutte l'arti meccaniche, e l'inventori loro, e li diversi modi, come s'usano in di-

qualities indicated. There are also carafes full of diverse liquids, a hundred and even three hundred years old, with which nearly all infirmities are cured.

On the inner wall of the third circuit every kind of herb and tree to be found in the world is represented. Moreover, specimens of each are grown in earthen vessels placed on the ravelins with explanations as to where they were first discovered, what their specific powers are, what their relation is to the stars, to metals, to parts of the body, and how they are used in medicine. On the outer wall are shown all manner of fish to be found in river, lake or ocean; their particular qualities; the way they live, breed, develop; their use; their correspondence to celestial and earthly things, to the arts, and to nature. I was astonished when I saw bishop fish, chain fish, nail fish, and starfish exactly resembling such things among us. There are sea urchins and molluscs, and all that is worth knowing about them is marvelously set down in word and picture.

On the inner wall of the fourth circuit are depicted all kinds of birds, their characteristics, sizes, and habits, and the Phoenix appears most real among them. On the outer wall are found all sorts of reptiles, serpents, dragons, worms, insects, flies, gnats, etc., with their habits, venoms, and attributes explained. These are more numerous than anyone thinks.

On the inner wall of the fifth circuit appear the perfect animals of the earth in such great variety as to amaze you. We do not know the thousandth part of them. Because these are large in body, they appear on the outer ravelins as well. How many horses alone there are of different kinds, all of them beautifully and accurately represented!

On the inner wall of the sixth circuit all the mechanical arts are displayed together with their inventors, their diverse forms, and their diverse uses in different

verse regioni del mondo. Nel di fuori vi son tutti l'inventori delle leggi e delle scienze e dell'armi. Trovai Moisè, Osiri, Giove, Mercurio, Macometto e altri assai; e in luoco assai onorato era Giesù Cristo e li dodici Apostoli, che ne tengono gran conto, Cesare, Alessandro, Pirro e tutti li Romani; onde io ammirato come sapeano quelle istorie, mi mostrâro che essi teneano di tutte nazioni lingua, e che mandavano apposta per il mondo ambasciatori, e s'informavano del bene e del male di tutti; e godeno assai in questo. Viddi che nella China le bombarde e le stampe fûro prima ch'a noi. Ci son poi li mastri di queste cose; e li figliuoli, senza fastidio, giocando, si trovano saper tutte le scienze istoricamente prima che abbin dieci anni.

Il Amore ha cura della generazione, con unir li maschi e le femine in modo che faccin buona razza; e si riden di noi che attendemo alla razza de cani e cavalli, e trascuramo la nostra. Tien cura dell'educazione, delle medicine, spezierie, del seminare e raccogliere li frutti, delle biade, delle mense e d'ogni altra cosa pertinente al vitto e vestito e coito, e ha molti maestri e maestre dedicate a queste arti.

Il Metafisico tratta tutti questi negozi con loro, chè senza lui nulla si fa, e ogni cosa la communicano essi quattro, e dove il Metafisico inchina, son d'accordo.

OSPITALARIO. Or dimmi degli offizi e dell'educazione e del modo come si vive; si è republica or monarchia o Stato di pochi.

GENOVESE. Questa è una gente ch'arrivò là dall'Indie, ed erano molti filosofi, che fuggîro la rovina di Mogori

parts of the world. On the outer wall all the founders of laws and of sciences and inventors of weapons appear. I found Moses, Osiris, Jupiter, Mercury, Muhammad, and many others there. In a place of special honor I saw Jesus Christ and the twelve Apostles, whom they hold in great regard. I saw Caesar, Alexander, Pyrrhus, and all the Romans. At this, when I marveled that they knew the histories of these men, they explained to me that they understood the languages of all of the nations and that they dispatched ambassadors throughout the world to learn what was both good and bad in each of them. They profit a good deal by doing this. I noted that explosives and printing were known in China before they became known among us. They have teachers for these things, and, without effort, merely while playing, their children come to know all the sciences pictorially before they are ten years old.

Love has charge of breeding and sees to the coupling of males and females who will produce healthy offspring. They laugh at us because we are careful about the breeding of dogs and horses while we pay no attention to our own breeding. He has charge of education, of medicines, of drugs, of the sowing and harvesting of crops, of the commissaries, and, in short, of all things pertaining to food, dress, and sexual intercourse. He has many men and women serving under him who are skilled in these functions.

The Metaphysician governs all matters through these three officers.[13] Without him nothing is done. Thus, everything is discussed among the four together, and what the Metaphysician decides all agree to.

HOSPITALER. Now tell me about their training and their duties and of the manner in which they live. Do they have a republic, a monarchy, or an oligarchy?

GENOESE. This is a people that came from India, many of them being philosophers, who fled before the

37

e d'altri predoni e tiranni; onde si risolsero di vivere alla filosofica in commune, si ben la communità delle donne non si usa tra le genti della provinzia loro; ma essi l'usano, ed è questo il modo. Tutte cose son communi; ma stan in man di offiziali le dispense, onde non solo il vitto, ma le scienze e onori e spassi son communi, ma in maniera che non si può appropriare cosa alcuna.

Dicono essi che tutta la proprietà nasce da far casa appartata, e figli e moglie propria, onde nasce l'amor proprio; chè, per sublimar a ricchezze o a dignità il figlio o lasciarlo erede, ognuno diventa o rapace publico, se non ha timore, sendo potente; o avaro e insidioso e ippocrita, si è impotente. Ma quando pèrdono l'amor proprio, resta il commune solo.

OSPITALARIO. Dunque nullo vorrà fatigare, mentre aspetta che l'altro fatichi, come Aristotile dice contra Platone.

GENOVESE. Io non so disputare, ma ti dico c'hanno tanto amore alla patria loro, che è una cosa stupenda, più che si dice delli Romani, quanto son più spropriati. E credo che li preti e monaci nostri, se non avessero li parenti e li amici, o l'ambizione de crescere più a dignità, sariano più spropriati e santi e caritativi con tutti.

OSPITALARIO. Dunque là non ci è amicizia, poichè non si fan piacere l'un l'altro.

GENOVESE. Anzi grandissima: perchè è bello a vedere, che tra loro non ponno donarsi cosa alcuna, perchè tutto hanno del commune; e molto guardano gli offiziali, che nullo abbia più che merita. Però quanto è bisogno tutti l'hanno. E l'amico si conosce tra loro nelle guerre, nell'infirmità, nelle scienze, dove s'aiutano e s'in-

depredations of the Tartars and other plunderers and tyrants, and they resolved to live in a philosophic community. Though community of wives was not practiced in the land they came from, they do practice it now, and in this manner: all things are held in common, but the dispensation of goods is left in the hands of officials. Not food alone, but arts, honors, and pleasure are also shared in common in such a way that no one can appropriate anything.

They claim that property comes into existence when men have separate homes with their children and wives. From this self-love is born; for in order to increase the wealth or dignity of his offspring or leave him heir to his goods, every man becomes publicly rapacious if he is strong and fearless, or avaricious, deceitful, and hypocritical if he is weak. When self-love is destroyed, only concern for the community remains.

HOSPITALER. Then no one must be willing to work, while he must expect everyone else to do so, as Aristotle charges in reply to Plato.[14]

GENOESE. I am unskilled in disputation, but I can tell you that the love they bear their country is an astonishing thing—as much greater than that of the Romans as their self-interest is less. And I believe that our priests and monks, if they had neither relatives nor friends nor ambition for higher office, would also be less given to self-interest, would be holier and more charitable to all.

HOSPITALER. Friendship then does not exist among them, since they cannot perform favors for one another.

GENOESE. On the contrary, it is very strong and a wonderful thing to behold. They cannot give gifts to one another because all is held in common and because the officials are careful to see that no one has more than he deserves, while everyone has all that he needs. But friendships develop in time of war, in sickness, and in the pursuit of knowledge wherein they help and en-

39

segnano l'un l'altro. E tutti li gioveni s'appellan frati, e quei che son quindici anni più di loro, padri, e quindici meno, figli. E poi vi stanno l'offiziali a tutte cose attenti, che nullo possa all'altro far torto nella fratellanza.

OSPITALARIO. E come?

GENOVESE. Di quante virtù noi abbiamo, essi hanno l'offiziale: ci è uno che si chiama Liberalità, uno Magninimità, uno Castità, uno Fortezza, uno Giustizia criminale o civile, un Solerzia, un Verità, Beneficenza, Gratitudine, Misericordia, ecc.; e a ciascuno di questi si elegge quello, che da fanciullo nelle scole si conosce inchinato a tal virtù. E però, non sendo tra loro latrocinii, nè assassinii, nè stupri e incesti, adultèri, delli quali noi ci accusamo, essi si accusano d'ingratitudine, di malignità, quando uno non vuol far piacere onesto, di bugia, che abborriscono più che la peste; e questi rei per pena son privati della mensa commune, o del commerzio delle donne, e d'alcuni onori, finchè pare al giudice, per ammendarli.

OSPITALARIO. Or dimmi, come fan gli offiziali?

GENOVESE. Questo non si può dire, se non sai la vita loro. Prima è da sapere che gli uomini e le donne vestono d'un modo atto a guerreggiare, benchè le donne hanno la sopravesta fin sotto al ginocchio e l'uomini sopra, e s'allevan tutti in tutte l'arti. Dopo li tre anni li fanciulli imparano la lingua e l'alfabeto nelle mura, caminando in quattro schiere; e quattro vecchi le guidano e insegnano, e poi li fan giocare e correre, per rin-

courage one another. Youths address each other as brothers; they address those who are their seniors by fifteen years or more as fathers and are, in turn, addressed by them as sons. Moreover, the officials watch over everything so that no one in the brotherhood can do harm to another.

HOSPITALER. How can this be?

GENOESE. For every virtue that exists among us, they have an official. They have one called Liberality, others called Magnanimity, Chastity, Fortitude, Criminal and Civil Justice, Zeal, Truth, Beneficence, Gratitude, Mercy, etc., and to each of these posts they elect someone who, from his schooldays on, showed a disposition toward the relevant virtue. Now since theft, murder, rape, incest, adultery—crimes of which some among us are guilty—do not exist among them, their offenses may only derive from ingratitude or malice, as when some person among them refuses to help another, or from lying, which they abhor more than the plague. Those who are guilty of these charges are punished by banishment from the common table or from intercourse with the opposite sex and are deprived of certain honors until the judge thinks they have been sufficiently punished.

HOSPITALER. Now tell me, how are their officials chosen?

GENOESE. This I cannot explain unless you know how they live. First of all, you must understand that their men and women dress in a manner suitable for combat, albeit the garment their women wear reaches below the knee and that of the men somewhat above.

Both sexes are trained in all pursuits. When they are three years old, children learn their alphabet and language, which are inscribed on the walls, by being led around them in four groups, each guided and instructed by an elder. Then they are made to run and play so as to

41

forzarli, e sempre scalzi e scapigli, fin alli sette anni, e li conducono nell'officine dell'arti, cositori, pittori, orefici, ecc.; e mirano l'inclinazione. Dopo li sette anni vanno alle lezioni delle scienze naturali, tutti; chè son quattro lettori della medesima lezione, e in quattro ore tutte quattro squadre si spediscono; perchè, mentre gli altri si esercitano il corpo, o fan li publici servizi, gli altri stanno alla lezione. Poi alli dieci tutti si mettono alle matematiche, medicine e altre scienze, e ci è continua disputa tra di loro e concorrenza; e quelli poi diventano offiziali di quella scienza, dove miglior profitto fanno, o di quell'arte meccanica, perchè ognuna ha il suo capo. E in campagna, nei lavori e nella pastura delle bestie pur vanno ad imparare; e quello è tenuto di più gran nobiltà, che più arti impara, e meglio le fa. Onde si ridono di noi che gli artefici appellamo ignobili, e diciamo nobili quelli, che null'arte imparano e stanno oziosi e tengono in ozio e lascivia tanti servitori con roina della republica.

Gli offiziali poi s'eleggono da quelli quattro capi, e dalli mastri di quell'arte, li quali molto bene sanno chi è più atto a quell'arte o virtù, in cui ha da reggere, e si propongono in consiglio, e ognuno oppone quel che sa di loro. Però non può essere Sole se non quello che sa tutte l'istorie delle genti e riti e sacrifizi e republiche e inventori di leggi e arti. Poi bisogna che sappia tutte l'arti meccaniche, perchè ogni due giorni se n'impara una, ma l'uso qui le fa saper tutte, e la pittura. E tutte le

gain strength. Barefoot and bareheaded until the age of seven, they are shown through the workshops of the various crafts, those of the needle-workers, painters, goldsmiths, etc., and they are watched so as to discover their inclination toward these crafts. After their seventh year they all take lessons in the natural sciences. Since there are four instructors for every lesson, all four groups may be taught a particular lesson in four hours. While some are engaged in physical exercises or in performing some public duty, others hear a lecture. Then at the age of ten they all study mathematics, medicine, and other sciences. There is continual debate and competition among them, and the one who shows the greatest proficiency in a particular science or mathematical art ultimately becomes the official in charge of it, for they have a leader for every study. They also go out into the countryside and learn the work of the fields and of pasturage. The one who learns the greatest number of skills and practices them best is judged to have the greatest nobility. Thus they laugh at us because we consider craftsmen ignoble and assign nobility to those who are ignorant of every craft and live in idleness, keeping a host of dissolute and idle servants about them to the great detriment of the state.

The officials are chosen by the four leaders [i.e., Sun, Pon, Sin and Mor] and by the teachers of the various arts. These know very well who is most suited for the particular task or virtue over which he is to preside. The candidates are nominated in council, and everyone present may tell what he knows against them. However, no one can be elected Sun unless he knows the history of all the peoples—their ceremonies, rites, and governments—and the inventors of all the arts and laws. He must moreover know all the mechanical arts, but each of these can be learned in two days, thanks to the fact that they are practiced and are graphically described on

scienze ha da sapere, matematiche, fisiche, astrologiche. Delle lingue non si cura, perchè ha l'interpreti, che son i grammatici loro. Ma più di tutti bisogna che sia metafisico e teologo, che sappia ben la radice e prova d'ogn'arte e scienza, e le similitudini e differenze delle cose, la Necessità, il Fato e l'Armonia del mondo, la Possanza, Sapienza e Amor divino e d'ogni cosa, e li gradi degli enti e corrispondenze loro con le cose celesti, terrestri e marine, e studia molto bene nei profeti e astrologia. Dunque si sa chi ha da esser Sole, e se non passa trentacinque anni, non arriva a tal grado; e questo offizio è perpetuo, mentre non si trova chi sappia più di lui e sia più atto al governo.

OSPITALARIO. E chi può saper tanto? Anzi, non può saper governare chi attende alle scienze.

GENOVESE. Io dissi a loro questo, e mi risposero: — Più certi semo noi, che un tanto letterato sa governare, che voi che sublimate l'ignoranti, pensando che siano atti perchè son nati signori, o eletti da fazione potente. Ma il nostro Sole sia pur tristo in governo: non sarà mai crudele, nè scelerato, nè tiranno un chi tanto sa. Ma sappiate che questo è argomento che può tra voi, dove pensate che sia dotto chi sa più grammatica e logica d'Aristotile o di questo o quello autore; al che ci vol sol memoria servile, onde l'uomo si fa inerte, perchè non contempla le cose ma li libri, e s'avvilisce l'anima in quelle cose morte; nè sa come Dio regga le cose, e gli usi

the walls besides. In addition, he must know the mathematical, physical, and astrological sciences. But he need not be concerned with languages since they have interpreters who serve as their grammarians. Above all, he must be a metaphysician and theologian who understands the theory and practice of every art and every science, the similitudes and differences among things, the Necessity, Fate, and Harmony of the world, the Power, Wisdom, and Love of God and of all things, the degrees of being and their correspondence to celestial, terrestrial, and marine things; and he must study astrology and the prophets carefully. They know whom they are to elect Sun, therefore, but no one can have the post unless he is thirty-five years old.[15] Once appointed, his tenure lasts until someone with greater knowledge and greater ability to rule is discovered.

HOSPITALER. But who can know so much? Besides, anyone who gives his attention to the sciences cannot know how to rule.

GENOESE. I told them this, and they replied: "We have greater certainty than you do that so learned a man does know how to govern, since it is your custom to exalt the ignorant either because they are nobly born or because some powerful faction chooses them. But our Sun, even if he were a bad ruler, would never be cruel or wicked or tyrannical, because he knows so much. You must understand that your argument is applicable to your own people rather than to ours because you term a man learned if he knows more than others do about Aristotle's grammar or logic or about some certain author—knowledge which requires only servile memory and which deprives the mind of vitality because it meditates upon books instead of things. Such inert stuff deadens the spirit which knows neither how God controls things nor how nature and nations operate. This

45

della natura e delle nazioni. Il che non può avvenire al nostro Sole, perchè non può arrivare a tante scienze chi non è scaltro d'ingegno ad ogni cosa, onde è sempre attissimo al governo. Noi pur sappiamo che chi sa una scienza sola, non sa quella nè l'altre bene; e che colui che è atto ad una sola, studiata in libro, è inerte e grosso. Ma non così avviene alli pronti d'ingegno e facili ad ogni conoscenza, come è bisogno che sia il Sole. E nella città nostra s'imparano le scienze con facilità tale, come vedi, che più in un anno qui si sa, che in diece o quindici tra voi, e mira in questi fanciulli.

Nel che io restai confuso per le ragioni sue e la prova di quelli fanciulli, che intendevano la mia lingua; perchè d'ogni lingua sempre hanno d'esser tre che la sappiano. E tra loro non ci è ozio nullo, se non quello che li fa dotti; chè però vanno in campagna a correre, a tirar dardi, sparar archibugi, seguitar fiere, lavorare, conoscer l'erbe, mo una schiera, mo un'altra di loro.

Li tre offiziali primi non bisogna che sappino se non quell'arti che all'offizio loro partengono. Onde sanno l'arti communi a tutti, istoricamente imparandole, e poi le proprie, dove più si dà uno che un altro: così il Potestà saperà l'arte cavalieresca, fabricar ogni sorte d'armi, cose di guerra, machine, arte militare, ecc. Ma tutti questi offiziali han d'essere filosofi, di più, e istorici, naturalisti e umanisti.

OSPITALARIO. Vorrei che dicessi l'offizi tutti, e li distinguessi; e s'è bisogno l'educazion commune.

cannot happen in the case of our Sun, for no one can master so many sciences unless he has a ready talent for all things. Therefore, such a person is always most able to rule. We also realize that anyone who knows only one science knows neither that one nor any other well and that anyone trained through books in one science alone is really worthless and ignorant. But this is not the case with those who are naturally apt and quick in every branch of knowledge, as our Sun must be. Moreover, in our city the sciences may be learned with such facility, as you can see, that more may be gained here in one year than in ten or fifteen among you.[16] For proof, just observe our children."

At these words, at the reasons he gave, and at the evidence furnished by the children I was amazed. For the children understood my language, each language being required study for three of them. Among them there is no idleness of any kind save that which they apply in learning. They go off, now one group and now another, into the countryside where they run, throw the spear, fire the harquebus, hunt animals, work with their hands, or study the plants.

The three major officials need not be well acquainted with any arts but those that apply to their office. About those arts that are common to all they have only a pictorial knowledge.[17] Their own art they know well, and each one devotes himself to his own. Thus Power is sure to know the art of horsemanship, how to make every kind of weapon, matters relating to warfare, engines, strategy, etc. But all three officials must moreover be philosophers, historians, naturalists, and humanists.

HOSPITALER. I wish you would tell me all their duties and distinguish between them and tell me also whether they need to have a common education.

GENOVESE. Sono prima le stanze communi, dormitori, letti e bisogni; ma ogni sei mesi si distingueno dalli mastri, chi ha da dormire in questo girone o in quell'altro, e nella stanza prima o seconda, notate per alfabeto.

Poi son l'arti communi agli uomini e donne, le speculative e meccaniche; con questa distinzione, che quelle dove ci va fatica grande e viaggio, le fan gli uomini, come arare, seminare, cogliere i frutti e pascer le pecore; però nell'aia, nella vendemia, nel formar il cascio e mungere si soleno le donne mandare, e nell'orti vicini alla città per erbe e servizi facili. Universalmente, le arti che si fanno sedendo e stando, per lo più son delle donne, come tessere, cuscire, tagliar i capelli e le barbe, la speziaria, fare tutte sorti di vestimenti; altro che l'arte del ferraro e delle armi. Pur chi è atta a pingere, non se le vieta. La musica è solo delle donne, perchè più dilettano, e de' fanciulli, ma non di trombe e tamburi. Fanno anche le vivande; apparecchiano le mense; ma il servire a tavola è proprio delli giovani, maschi e femine, finchè son di vint'anni.

Hanno in ogni girone le publiche cucine e le dispense della robba. E ad ogni officio soprastante è un vecchio e una vecchia, che comandano e han potestà di battere o far battere da altri li negligenti e disobedienti, e notano ognuno e ognuna in che esercizio meglio riesce. Tutta la gioventù serve alli vecchi che passano quarant'anni; ma il mastro e maestra han cura la sera, quando vanno a dormire, e la mattina di mandar alli servizi di quelli a chi tocca, uno o due ad ogni stanza, ed essi giovani si servono tra loro, e chi ricusa, guai a lui! Vi son prime e seconde mense: d'una parte mangiano le donne, dall'altra gli uomini, e stanno come in refettori di frati. Si fa

GENOESE. First of all, there are common rooms, dormitories, beds, and toilets, and every six months the masters decide who is to be in that circuit, who is to occupy this or that room, each of which is identified by a letter of the alphabet.

Men and women perform the same tasks, whether of a mental or mechanical nature. But one distinction is observed, and that is that such tasks as involve hard work or a good deal of walking, like plowing, sowing, harvesting, sheep herding, are performed by the men. Threshing, grape gathering, cheese making, milking, tending to the kitchen gardens, and other light duties, on the other hand, are usually assigned to women. These include weaving, sewing, barbering, pharmacy, every kind of clothes making, but exclude the work of the blacksmith or of the arms maker. If a woman has skill in painting, she is not forbidden to pursue it. Music, except for the playing of trumpet and drums, is reserved to women and children since they give most pleasure by it. Women also prepare food and lay the tables, but only boys and girls up to the age of twenty wait on tables.

There are public kitchens and supply rooms in every circuit. Every function is presided over by an elderly man and woman who have authority to administer beatings (or have them administered by others) to anyone who is negligent or disobedient. They also take note of those who best do their work. All of the young folks are required to attend to those who are over forty years of age. In the morning and again in the evening when it is time to retire, the master and mistress assign them to the particular duties they are to perform, one or two going to each room. These young folks also serve each other, and woe to anyone who refuses to obey! There are two servings of every meal. The women sit on one side and the men on the other, in the manner of

senza strepito, e un sempre legge a tavola, cantando, e spesso l'offiziale parla sopra qualche passo della lezione. È una dolce cosa vedersi servire di tanta bella gioventù, in abito succinto, così a tempo, e vedersi a canto tanti amici, frati, figli e madri vivere con tanto rispetto e amore.

Si dona a ciascuno, secondo il suo esercizio, piatto di pitanza e minestra, frutti, cascio; e le medici hanno cura di dire alli cochi in quel giorno, qual sorte di vivanda conviene, e quale alli vecchi e quale alli giovani e quale all'ammalati. Gli offiziali hanno miglior parte; questi mandano spesso della loro a tavola a chi più si ha fatto onore la mattina nelle lezioni e dispute di scienze e armi, e questo si stima per grande onore e favore. E nelle feste fanno cantar una musica pur in tavola; e perchè tutti mettemo mano alli servizi, mai non si trova che manchi cosa alcuna. Son vecchi savi soprastanti a chi cucina e alli refettori, e stimano assai la nettezza nelle strade, nelle stanze e nellii vasi e nelle vestimenta e nella persona.

Vesteno dentro camisa bianca di lino, poi un vestito, ch'è giubbone e calza insieme, senza pieghe e spaccato per mezzo, dal lato e di sotto, e poi imbottonato. E arriva la calza insino al tallone, a cui si pone un pedale grande come un bolzacchino, e la scarpa sopra. E son ben attillate, che quando si spogliano la sopraveste, si scerneno tutte le fattezze della persona. Si mutano le vesti quattro volte varie, quando il Sole entra in Cancro e Capricorno, Ariete e Libra. E, secondo la complessione e procerità, sta al Medico di distribuirle col Ve-

monks at refectory. They eat in silence, but someone always reads to them, intoning aloud, and often an official will enlarge upon a particular passage of the reading. It is indeed a wonderful thing to be served with such promptitude by so many handsome youths, apparelled in short belted tunics, and to be surrounded by so many friends, brothers, mothers, and children, all living together in mutual love and respect.

Each is served according to his needs with a main dish, some soup, fruit, and cheese. The physicians have the duty of informing the cooks every day as to what kind of food is the most suitable to prepare respectively for the old, the young, and the ill. The officials receive the most choice portions, and they often order that a part of the food from their table be served to some one or other who distinguished himself that morning in a lesson or discussion or military exercise. The recipient regards this as a singular honor and mark of favor. On feast days there is singing at table. Because everyone takes a hand in providing, nothing is ever lacking. Certain wise elders are assigned to supervise the kitchens and dining halls, and they insist upon cleanliness everywhere—in the streets, the chambers, the utensils, in body, and in dress.

The people dress in undershirts of white linen over which they wear a suit combining jacket and trousers in one piece. This has no folds, but there are splits on the side and beneath, which are closed with buttons. The trouser part reaches to the heels, which are covered with heavy socks and shoes. All the garments are neatly fitted, and when the suit is removed, the outline of the body is clearly discernible. Four times each year, when the sun enters Cancer, Capricorn, Aries, and Libra,[18] the people change to other outfits, which are distributed to them according to shape and size by the Keeper of the Wardrobe of each circuit and by the physician working

stiario di ciascun girone. Ed è cosa mirabile che in un punto hanno quante vesti vogliono, grosse, sottili, secondo il tempo. Veston tutti di bianco, e ogni mese si lavan le vesti con sapone, o bucato quelle di tela.

Tutte le stanze sottane sono officine, cucine, granari, guardarobbe, dispense, refettori, lavatori; ma si lavano nelle pile delli chiostri. L'acqua si getta per le latrine o per canali, che vanno a quelle. Hanno in tutte le piazze delli gironi le lor fontane, che tirano l'acque dal fondo solo con muover un legno, onde esse spicciano per li canali. Vi è acqua sorgente molta e nelle conserve, a cui vanno le piogge per li canali delle case, passando per arenosi acquedotti. Si lavano le persone loro spesso, secondo il maestro e 'l medico ordina. L'arti si fanno tutte nei chiostri di sotto, e le speculative di sopra, dove sono le pitture, e nel tempio si leggono negli atri di fuora. Son orologi di sole e di squille per tutti i gironi, e banderole per saper i venti.

OSPITALARIO. Or dimmi della generazione.

GENOVESE. Nulla femina si sottopone al maschio, se non arriva a dicinov'anni, nè il maschio si mette alla generazione inanti alli vintiuno, e più si è di complessione bianco. Nel tempo inanti ad alcuno è lecito il coito con le donne sterili o pregne, per non far in vaso indebito; e le maestre matrone con li seniori della generazione han cura di provederli, secondo a loro è detto in secreto da quelli più molestati da Venere. Li provedono, ma non lo fanno senza far parola al maestro maggiore, che è un gran medico, e sottostà ad Amore, prencipe

with him. It is wonderful to observe that they have ready at hand as many clothes as are needed, whether heavy or light, just as the season requires. They all dress in white, and once each month wash their suits with soap and bleach their linens.

All of the rooms on the ground floors are used as kitchens, granaries, wardrobes, supply stations, refectories, and washrooms. The washing is done in stone basins located in the cloisters. The dirty water is thrown into the latrines or into channels that lead to them. There are fountains in the plazas of every circuit from which, by simply moving a wooden bar, one may draw the water which then flows along the channels. There is an abundance of water and there are cisterns, the latter being used to collect rain water from the roof gutters. This is then filtered to the cisterns through sand-laden conduits. The people wash often, according as the chief or physician orders. The arts and crafts are practiced in the lower cloisters; the more speculative pursuits are carried on in those above, where the paintings are located; the porches of the temple are used for reading. In every circle there are both sundials and mechanical clocks with chimes as well as pennons to indicate wind direction.

HOSPITALER. Now tell me about their procreating.

GENOESE. No female ever submits to a male until she is nineteen years of age, nor does any male seek to have children until he is twenty-one or, if he is pale and delicate, even older. Before that age some of them are permitted to have intercourse with barren or pregnant women so as to avoid illicit usages. The matrons and seniors in charge of procreation are responsible for providing in accordance with what those who are most troubled by Venus reveal to them in secret. They provide, but never without first having spoken with their chief, an eminent physician who is directly responsible

offiziale. Se si trovano in sodomia, son vituperati, e li fan portare due giorni legata al collo una scarpa, significando che pervertîro l'ordine e posero li piedi in testa, e la seconda volta crescen la pena finchè diventa capitale. Ma chi si astiene fin a ventun anno d'ogni coito è celebrato con alcuni onori e canzoni.

Perchè quando si esercitano alla lotta, come i Greci antichi, son nudi tutti, maschi e femine, li mastri conoscono chi è impotente o no al coito, e quali membra con quali si confanno. E così, sendo ben lavati, si donano al coito ogni tre sere; e non accoppiano se non le femine grandi e belle alli grandi e virtuosi, e le grasse a' macri, e le macre alli grassi, per far temperie. La sera vanno i fanciulli e conciano i letti, e poi vanno a dormire, secondo ordina il mastro e la maestra. Nè si pongon al coito, se non quando hanno digerito, e prima fanno orazione, e hanno belle statue di uomini illustri, dove le donne mirano. Poi escono alla finestra, e pregono Dio del Cielo, che li doni prole buona. E dormeno in due celle, sparti fin a quell'ora che si han da congiungere, e allora va la maestra, e apre l'uscio dell'una e l'altra cella. Questa ora è determinata dall'Astrologo e Medico; e si forzan sempre di pigliar tempo, che Mercurio e Venere siano orientali dal Sole in casa benigna, e che sian mirati da Giove di buono aspetto e da Saturno e Marte così il Sole come la Luna, che spesso sono afete. E per lo più

to Love, the principal officer. Those who commit sodomy are disgraced and are made to walk about for two days with a shoe tied to their necks as a sign that they perverted natural order, putting their feet where the head belongs. With each repetition of the offense the sentence is increased until finally the punishment is death. On the other hand, those who abstain from every form of sexual intercourse until they reach twenty-one are honored, and odes are written in their praise.

Since both males and females, in the manner of the ancient Greeks, are completely naked when they engage in wrestling exercises, their teachers may readily distinguish those who are able to have intercourse from those who are not and can determine whose sexual organs may best be matched with whose. Consequently, every third night, after they have all bathed, the young people are paired off for intercourse. Tall handsome girls are not matched with any but tall brave men, while fat girls are matched with thin men and thin girls with fat ones, so as to avoid extremes in their offspring. On the appointed evening, the boys and girls prepare their beds and go to bed where the matron and senior direct them. Nor may they have intercourse until they have completely digested their food and have said their prayers. There are fine statues of illustrious men that the women gaze upon. Then both male and female go to a window to pray to the God of Heaven for good issue. They sleep in separate neighboring cells until they are to have intercourse. At the proper time, the matron goes around and opens the cell doors. The exact hour when this must be done is determined by the Astrologer and the Physician, who always endeavor to choose a time when Mercury and Venus are oriental to the Sun in a benefic house and are seen by Jupiter, Saturn, and Mars with benefic aspect. So too by the sun and the moon that are often aphetic.[19] Most frequently they seek a

vogliono Vergine in ascendente; ma assai si guardano che Saturno o Marte non stiano in angolo, perchè tutti quattro angoli con opposizioni e quadrati infettano, e da essi angoli è la radice della virtù vitale e della sorte, dependente dall'armonia del tutto con le parti. Non si curano di satellizio, ma solo degli aspetti buoni. Ma il satellizio solo nella fondazione della città e della legge ricercano, che però non abbia prencipe Marte o Saturno, se non con buone disposizioni. E han per peccato li generatori non trovarsi mondi tre giorni avanti di coito e d'azioni prave, e di non esser devoti al Creatore. Gli altri, che per delizia o per servire alla necessità si donano al coito con sterili o pregne o con donne di poco valore, non osservan queste sottigliezze. E gli offiziali, che son tutti sacerdoti, e li sapienti non si fanno generatori, se non osservano molti giorni più condizioni; perchè essi, per la molta speculazione, han debole lo spirito animale, e non trasfondono il valor della testa, perchè pensano sempre a qualche cosa; onde trista razza fanno. Talchè si guarda bene, e si donano questi a donne vive, gagliarde e belle; e gli uomini fantastichi e capricciosi a donne grasse, temperate, di costumi blandi. E dicono che la purità della complessione, onde le virtù fruttano, non si può acquistare con arte, e che difficilmente senza disposizion naturale può la virtù morale allignare, e che gli uomini di mala natura per timor della legge fanno bene, e, quella cessante, struggon la republica con manifesti o segreti modi. Però tutto lo studio principale deve essere

time when Virgo is in the ascendant, but they take great care to see that Saturn and Mars are not in the angles, because all four angles, with oppositions and quadratures, are harmful; and from these springs the root of vital power and of fate, which are dependent upon the harmony of the whole in relation to its parts.[20] They are not concerned about the influence of satellites but about favorable aspects alone. They reckon the influence of satellites only in matters relating to the foundation of the city and the law, seeing to it that, if Mars or Saturn is the ruler, it shall be beneficently disposed.[21] Intended parents are deemed to have sinned unless they have avoided coitus and acts of impurity for three days before mating and unless they have shown devotion to their Creator. Other males who indulge in sexual intercourse with sterile or pregnant women or with women of scant worth, whether for pleasure or for need, need not observe these subtleties. The officials, all of whom are priests, and the learned do not try to procreate without first submitting to numerous conditions and restrictions stretching over many days. The reason for this is that those who are much given to speculation tend to be deficient in animal spirits and fail to bestow their intellectual powers upon their progeny because they are always thinking of other matters. Thus they produce offspring of poor quality. As a consequence, they take care to mate with energetic, spirited, handsome women. Men who have a flighty, capricious disposition are matched with women who are fat, even-tempered, and gentle. The Solarians say that a pure nature wherein virtues thrive cannot be acquired through study and application, that moral virtue is fostered only with difficulty where there is no natural disposition to favor it, that ill-natured men do good only through fear of the law, and that when this fails, they destroy the state by open and covert means. Care in mating, therefore, is a

57

nella generazione, e mirar li meriti naturali, e non la dote o la fallace nobiltà.

Se alcune di queste donne non concipeno con uno, le mettono con altri; se poi si trova sterile, si può accomunare, ma non ha l'onor delle matrone in consiglio della generazione e nella mensa e nel tempio; e questo lo fanno perchè essa non procuri la sterilità per lussuriare. Quelle che hanno conceputo, per quindici giorni non si esercitano; poi fanno leggeri esercizi per rinforzar la prole e aprir le meati del nutrimento a quella. Partorito che hanno, esse stesse allevano i figli in luochi comuni, per due anni lattando e più, secondo pare al Fisico. Dopo si smamma la prole, e si dona in guardia delle mastre, se son femine, o delli maestri, con gli altri fanciulli; e qui si esercitano all'alfabeto, a caminare, correre, lottare e alle figure istoriate; e han vesti di color vario e bello. Alli sette anni si donano alle scienze naturali, e poi all'altre, secondo pare agli offiziali, e poi si mettono in meccanica. Ma li figli di poco valore si mandano alle ville, e, quando riescono, poi si riducono alla città. Ma per lo più, sendo generati nella medesima costellazione, li contemporanei son di virtù consimili e di fattezze e di costumi. E questa è concordia stabile nella republica, e s'amano grandemente e aiutano l'un l'altro.

Li nomi loro non si mettono a caso, ma dal Metafisico, secondo la proprietà, come usavan li Romani:

matter of major concern. The aim should be to improve natural endowments, not to provide doweries or false titles of nobility.

If a woman fails to conceive when coupled with a particular man, she is matched with another. If she proves sterile, she is allowed to have intercourse with anyone; but in such a case, she is not granted equal privileges with the matrons in the Council on Procreation, nor at table, nor at temple. This is intended to discourage any woman from making herself sterile in order to become a wanton. When a woman has conceived, she avoids all exercise for fifteen days. Then she begins to take only light exercise so as to strengthen the unborn infant and open to it the channels of nourishment. Once it is born, the mother suckles it and cares for it herself in a public nursery for a period of two years or longer, according to the judgment of the Physical Scientist. After being weaned, the child is put into the care of teachers—male or female, according to the child's sex. Here, in the company of other children, he studies the alphabet and the paintings on the walls and also learns to walk, run, and wrestle. Children wear clothes of various pleasant colors. At the age of seven they are directed to the natural sciences and then to the other sciences as the officials determine. After this, they take up the mechanical arts. Those who demonstrate little ability are sent out into the country. When they improve, they are brought back to the city. But in general, since those of the same age are all born under the same constellation, they tend to be alike in ability, habits, and appearance. This accounts for the concord and stability in the state and encourages the citizens to love and help each other.

It is not mere chance that determines the name of a person, for the Metaphysician himself assigns it according to some characteristic, as the Romans did. Thus one

onde altri si chiamano il Bello, altri il Nasuto, altri il Peduto, altri Bieco, altri Crasso, ecc.; ma quando poi diventano valenti nell'arte loro o fanno qualche prova in guerra, s'aggiunge il cognome dall'arte, come Pittor Magno, Aureo, Eccellente, Gagliardo, dicendo: Crasso Aureo, ecc.; o pur dall'atto dicendo: Crasso Forte, Astuto, Vincitore, Magno, Massimo, ecc., e dal nemico vinto, come Africano, Asiano, Tosco, ecc.; Manfredi, Tortelio dall'aver superato Manfredi o Tortelio o simili altri. E questi cognomi s'aggiungono dall'offiziali grandi, e si donano con una corona conveniente all'atto o arte sua, con applauso e musica. E si vanno a perdere per questi applausi, perchè oro e argento non si stima, se non come materia di vasi o di guarnimenti communi a tutti.

OSPITALARIO. Non ci è gelosia tra loro o dolore a chi non sia fatto generatore o quel che ambisce?

GENOVESE. Signor no, perchè a nullo manca il necessario loro quanto al gusto; e la generazione è osservata religiosamente per ben publico, non privato, ed è bisogno stare al detto dell'offiziali. Platone disse che si dovean gabbare li pretendenti a belle donne immeritamente, con far uscir la sorte destramente secondo il merito; il che qui non bisogna far con inganno di ballotte per contentarsi delle brutte i brutti, perchè tra loro non ci è bruttezza; chè, esercitandosi esse donne, diventano di color vivo e di membra forti e grandi, e nella gagliardia e vivezza e grandezza consiste la beltà appresso a loro. Però è pena della vita imbellettarsi la faccia o portar pianelle, o vesti con le code per coprir i piedi di legno; ma non averiano commodità manco di far

is called Pulcher, another is called Naso, another Pedutus, another Torvus, another Crassus, etc. When he has gained skill in some particular craft or has given some proof of himself in war, he is given an appropriate surname in addition—Pictor Magnus, Aureus, Excellens, Validus—so as to form Crassus Aureus, etc.; or if based upon some action: Crassus Fortis, Astutus, Victor, Magnus, Maximus, etc.; or if based upon some conquest: Africanus, Asianus, Tuscus, etc.; or if based upon a defeated enemy: Manfredus or Tortelius, assuming he has defeated one of these. These surnames, along with appropriate coronals, are bestowed publicly by the chief officials to the sound of music and applause. To gain such approval citizens are willing to risk their lives, since neither gold nor silver is much regarded except as the material out of which to make vessels and ornaments that are common to everyone.

HOSPITALER. Is there no jealousy among them or hurt at not being chosen for parenthood? Is there no coveting?

GENOESE. Sir, there is none, for no necessity to their pleasure is lacking, and the rules governing procreation are religiously observed for public, not for private ends. Moreover, there is the need to obey official orders. Plato said that it would be necessary to trick undeserving men who felt they had a right to beautiful women by managing the drawing of lots in such a way that only the deserving would win such women.[22] But in the City of the Sun there is no need to cheat so as to match ugly men with ugly women, for there are no ugly ones among them. By exercising, the women develop lively complexions and large, strong limbs; and among these people tallness, liveliness, and strength are the attributes of beauty. It is a capital offense for women to use cosmetics, however, or to wear high heels and gowns with trains to cover the heels. But actually there is no

61

questo, perchè chi ci li daria? E dicono che questo abuso in noi viene dall'ozio delle donne, che le fa scolorite e fiacche e piccole; e però han bisogno di colori e alte pianelle, e di farsi belle per tenerezza, e così guastano la propria complessione e della prole. Di più, s'uno s'innamora di qualche donna, è lecito tra loro parlare, far versi, scherzi, imprese di fiori e di piante. Ma se si guasta la generazione, in nullo modo si dispensa tra loro il coito, se non quando ella è pregna o sterile. Però non si conosce tra loro se non amor d'amicizia per lo più, non di concupiscenza ardente.

La robba non si stima, perchè ognuno ha quanto li bisogna, salvo per segno d'onore. Onde agli eroi ed eroisse la republica fa certi doni, in tavola o in feste publiche, di ghirlande o di vestimenta belle fregiate; benchè tutti di bianco il giorno e nella città, ma di notte e fuor della città vestono a rosso, o di seta o di lana. Abborreno il color nero, come feccia delle cose, e però odiano i Giapponesi, amici di quello. La superbia è tenuta per gran peccato, e si punisce un atto di superbia in quel modo che l'ha commesso. Onde nullo reputa viltà servire in mensa, in cucina o altrove, ma lo chiamano imparare; e dicono che così è onore al piede caminare, come all'occhio guardare; onde chi è deputato a qualche offizio, lo fa come cosa onoratissima, e non tengono schiavi, perchè essi bastano a se stessi, anzi soverchiano. Ma noi non così, perchè in Napoli son da trecento milia anime, e non faticano cinquanta milia; e questi pa-

need to forbid these things, for where could they get them? They claim that such abuses exist among us because of the idleness of our women, which makes them pale, fragile, and short and creates a need for artificial coloring, high heels, and beauty care. Thus our women ruin their constitutions and that of their children as well. If a man becomes enamored of a woman, he may speak and jest with her, send her verses, and make emblems out of flowers and branches for her. But if his having intercourse with her is deemed undesirable by reason of the offspring that might result, it will by no means be permitted unless she is already pregnant or is sterile. As a result, only loving friendship, rather than concupiscent ardor, is recognized among them.

Possessions, save as marks of honor, are not highly regarded since everyone has as many as he needs. But the state makes gifts to its heroes and heroines on occasions when the people are assembled in the dining halls or when there is a holiday. These gifts may be garlands or they may be cloaks of silk or wool that are beautifully ornamented, in spite of the fact that all the people wear white in the city during the day and red, either silk or wool, in the country and at night. They abhor black as though it were something foul; consequently, they despise the Japanese for favoring this color. Pride is regarded as a great sin, and it is punished after the manner in which it is committed. Therefore, no one considers it disgraceful to wait at tables or to serve in the kitchen or elsewhere. Such work they call learning, and they say that it is as honorable for the feet to walk as for the eyes to see. Thus anyone who is assigned any particular task performs it as though it were a high honor. They keep no slaves, since they are sufficient unto themselves and more. But it is not so with us, for there are three hundred thousand souls in Naples and not fifty thousand of them work,[23] and these work so hard that they destroy

tiscono fatica assai e si struggono; e l'oziosi si perdono anche per l'ozio, avarizia, lascivia e usura, e molta gente guastano, tenendoli in servitù e povertà, o fandoli partecipi di lor vizi, talchè manca il servizio publico, e non si può il campo, la milizia o l'arte fare, se non male e con stento. Ma tra loro, partendosi l'offizi a tutti e le arti e fatiche, non tocca faticar quattro ore il giorno per uno; sì ben tutto il resto è imparare giocando, disputando, leggendo, insegnando, caminando, e sempre con gaudio. E non s'usa gioco che si faccia sedendo, nè scacchi, nè dadi, nè carte o simili, ma ben la palla, il pallone, rollo, lotta, tirar palo, dardo, archibugio.

Dicono ancora che la povertà grande fa gli uomini vili, astuti, ladri, insidiosi, fuorasciti, bugiardi, testimoni falsi; e le ricchezze insolenti, superbi, ignoranti, traditori, disamorati, presumitori di quel che non sanno. Però la communità tutti li fa ricchi e poveri: ricchi, ch'ogni cosa hanno e possedono; poveri, perchè non s'attaccano a servire alle cose, ma ogni cosa serve a loro. E molto laudano in questo le religioni della cristianità e la vita dell'Apostoli.

OSPITALARIO. È bella cosa questa e santa; ma quella delle donne communi pare dura e ardua. S. Clemente Romano dice che le donne pur sian communi, ma la glosa intende quanto all'ossequio, non al letto, e Tertulliano consente alla glosa; chè i Cristiani antichi tutto ebbero commune, altro che le mogli, ma queste pur fûro communi nell'ossequio.

themselves. Meanwhile, the idle ruin themselves in pursuing idleness, avarice, lasciviousness, and usury; and they ruin still others by keeping them in impoverished servitude or by making them parties to their own vices. As a consequence, the public services are not sufficiently attended to. The tasks of the fields, of the camps, and of the crafts are badly performed even with great effort. In the City of the Sun, on the other hand, no one need work more than four hours each day because official duties, craftwork, and labor are equitably distributed.[24] The people spend the remaining hours in learning by playing games or debating or reading or teaching or walking—all of these with pleasure. But they do not indulge in any game that can be played sitting down. Chess, dice, cards they avoid. Instead they play catch or soccer, roll the discus,[25] wrestle, or practice with the javelin, the bow, or the harquebus.

They assert that extreme poverty makes men liars, false witnesses, thieves, outlaws—cunning, cowardly, and deceitful—while wealth makes them insolent, haughty, ignorant, disaffected, treacherous, and presumptuous. But public ownership of goods makes them all rich and poor at the same time—rich in that they possess everything, poor in that they do not have possessions to serve, while all possessions serve them. On this point they have high praise for the tenets of Christianity and for the lives of the Apostles.

HOSPITALER. This is a beautiful and holy thing, but as regards the community of women, that is difficult to accept. The Roman St. Clement also says there should be community of women, but the gloss interprets this to refer to obedience, not to the bed. Tertullian approves the gloss, for the early Christians held all things except wives in common, though these too were held in common with regard to obedience.[26]

GENOVESE. Io non so di questo; so ben che essi han l'ossequio commune delle donne e 'l letto, ma non sempre, se non per generare. E credo che si possano ingannare ancora; ma essi si difendono con Socrate, Catone, Platone e altri. Potria stare che lasciassero quest'uso un giorno, perchè nelle città soggette a loro non accomunano se non le robbe, e le donne quanto all'ossequio e all'arti, ma non al letto; e questo l'ascrivono all'imperfezione di quelli che non han filosofato. Però vanno spiando di tutte nazioni l'usanze, e sempre migliorano; e quando sapranno le ragioni vive del Cristianesmo, provate con miracoli, consentiranno, perchè son dolcissimi. Ma fin mo trattano naturalmente senza fede rivelata; nè ponno a più sormontare.

Di più questo è bello, che fra loro non ci è difetto che faccia l'uomo ozioso, se non l'età decrepita, quando serve solo per consiglio. Ma chi è zoppo serve alle sentinelle con gli occhi; chi non ha occhi serve a carminar la lana e levar il pelo dal nervo delle penne per li matarazzi; chi non ha mani, ad altro esercizio; e se un solo membro ha, con quello serve; ma questi stanno, se non fûro illustrissimi per la città, nelle ville, e son governati bene, e son spie che avvisano alla republica ogni cosa.

OSPITALARIO. Di' mo della guerra; chè poi dell'arti e vitto mi dirai, poi delle scienze, e al fine della religione.

GENOVESE. Il Potestà tiene sotto di sè un offiziale dell'armi, un altro dell'artellaria, un delli cavalieri, un delli ingegneri; e ognuno di questi ha sotto di sè molti

GENOESE. I don't know about that. However, I do know that they share their women with respect to both obedience and the bed, but not always, only when they are to have children. I believe they could be in error, but they defend the practice by citing Socrates, Cato, Plato, and others.[27] It may be that one day they will abandon this custom, for in the cities that are subject to them goods are shared in common and women too, but only in regard to obedience and work, not to the bed; and this exemption they attribute to the imperfection of those who are unlearned in philosophy. But the City of the Sun sends out spies to all nations to learn their customs and is continually improving its own. When the people learn the living truths of Christianity, proved by miracles, they will submit to them, for they are very pliant people.[28] But so far they rely upon nature without the revealed faith and cannot go beyond it.

Also admirable is the fact that among them no physical defect justifies a man's being idle except the decrepitude of age, at which time of life he is still useful as an adviser. If a man is lame, his eyes make him useful as a sentinel; if he is blind, he may still card wool or pluck the down from feathers to stuff mattresses; if he has lost his hands, he can still serve some purpose. If he has but one sound limb remaining, he gives service with that, but all such people, unless they have won renown in the city, are kept in the countryside. All are well supervised, and there are informers who report to the state about everything.

HOSPITALER. Tell me now about warfare. Then you can tell me about their arts, their food, their sciences, and finally about their religion.

GENOESE. Serving under Power, there is an officer in charge of infantry, another in charge of artillery, another in charge of cavalry, and still another in charge of engineers. Each of them in turn has many officers below

mastri di quell'arte. Ma di più ci sono gli atleti, che a tutti insegnano l'esercizio della guerra. Questi sono attempati, prudenti capitani, che esercitano li gioveni di dodici anni in suso all'arme; benchè prima nella lotta e correre e tirar pietre erano avvezzi da mastri inferiori. Or questi l'insegnano a ferire, a guadagnar l'inimico con arte, a giocar di spada, di lancia, a saettare, a cavalcare, a sequire, a fuggire, a star nell'ordine militare. E le donne pure imparano queste arti sotto maestre e mastri loro, per quando fusse bisogno aiutar gli uomini nelle guerre vicine alla città; e, se venisse assalto, difendono le mura. Onde ben sanno sparar l'archibugio, far balle, gittar pietre, andar incontro. E si sforzano tôr da loro ogni timore, e hanno gran pene quei che mostran codardia. Non temono la morte, perchè tutti credono l'immortalità dell'anima, e che, morendo, s'accompagnano con li spiriti buoni o rei, secondo li meriti. Benchè essi siano stati Bragmani pittagorici, non credono trasmigrazione d'anima, se non per qualche giudizio di Dio. Nè s'astengono di ferir il nimico ribello della ragione, che non merita esser uomo.

Fanno la mostra ogni dui mesi, e ogni giorno ci è l'esercizio dell'arme, o in campagna, cavalcando, o dentro, e una lezione d'arte militare, e fanno sempre leggere l'istorie di Cesare, d'Alessandro, di Scipione e d'Annibale, e poi dànno il giudizio loro quasi tutti, dicendo: — Qui fecero bene, qui male—; e poi risponde il mastro e determina.

OSPITALARIO. Con chi fan le guerre? e per che causa, se son tanto felici?

him who are masters of their particular specialty. In addition there are the athletes who provide military training for all the people. These are prudent veteran officers who exercise youths of twelve years and upward in warfare, after they have already been taught to wrestle, run, and throw by inferior officers. Beginning at the age of twelve, youths are taught to strike; to overcome the enemy by craft; to use the sword, the spear, the bow; to ride, pursue, retreat, and maintain military formation. The women are also taught these skills by their masters and mistresses in the event that they should be needed to help the fighting men in the vicinity of the city. In case of an assault, they can defend the walls. Thus they know how to handle the harquebus, make shot, fling weights, and make sallies. They try hard to put away all fear, and they are severely punished if they show cowardice. But they are not afraid of dying, for everyone believes in the immortality of the soul and that after death he will, according to his merits, join the company of the good or wicked spirits. Though they are descended from Pythagorean Brahmans,[29] they do not believe in the transmigration of souls, except possibly through some act of Divine judgment. Nor do they refrain from wounding enemies who are rebels to reason and, as such, do not deserve to be called men.

Every two months there is a military review, and every day there are troop exercises either on horseback in the countryside or within the walls. There is also a daily lesson in the art of war. They continually study the histories of Caesar, Alexander, Scipio, and Hannibal and express their opinions, saying "here they did well, here badly." Then the instructor responds and passes judgment.

HOSPITALER. If they are so happy, with whom do they make war and for what reason?

69

GENOVESE. Se mai non avessero guerra, pure s'esercitano all'arte di guerra e alla caccia per non impoltronire e per quel che potria succedere. Di più, vi son quattro regi nell'isola, li quali han grande invidia della felicità loro, perchè li popoli desiderariano vivere come questi Solari, e vorriano star più soggetti ad essi, che non a' proprii regi. Onde spesso loro è mossa guerra, sotto color d'usurpar confini e di viver empiamente, perchè non sequeno le superstizioni di Gentili, nè dell'altri Bragmani; e spesso li fan guerra, come ribelli che prima erano soggetti. E con tutto questo perdono sempre. Or essi Solari, subito che patiscono preda, insulto o altro disonore, o son travagliati l'amici loro, o pure son chiamati d'alcune città tiranneggiate come liberatori, essi si mettono a consiglio, e prima s'inginocchiano a Dio e pregano che li faccia ben consigliarsi, poi s'esamina il merito del negozio, e così si bandisce la guerra. Mandano un sacerdote detto il Forense: costui dimanda a' nemici che rendano il tolto o lascino la tirannia; e se quelli negano, li bandiscono la guerra, chiamando Dio delle vendette in testimonio contra chi ha il torto; e si quelli prolungano il negozio, non li dànno tempo, si è re, più d'un'ora, si è republica, tre ore a deliberar la risposta, per non esser burlati; e così si piglia la guerra, se quelli son contumaci alla ragione. Ma dopo ch'è pigliata, ogni cosa esequisce il locotenente del Potestà; ed esso comanda senza consiglio d'altri, ma, si è cosa di momento, domanda il Amor e 'l Sapienza e 'l Sole. Si propone in consiglio grande, dove entra tutto il popolo

GENOESE. Even if they should have no wars, they would practice the military arts as well as hunting in order to shun indolence and be prepared for the unexpected. But there are four kings on the island who are deeply envious of the felicity the City of the Sun enjoys because their subjects would like to live like the Solarians and pay homage to them rather than to their own kings. Thus, under pretense that their borders have been violated or that the City of the Sun is impious in not observing the superstitions of other lands and of the other Brahmans, these kings frequently make war upon it. Sometimes they attack it, claiming that it is a subject city that has revolted. Yet despite all this they always lose. Now as soon as the Solarians are attacked, insulted, or dishonored in some way, when their allies are put upon, or when they are called to liberate some city that is being tyrannized, they summon a council. After having kneeled and prayed God to guide their deliberations, the council members examine the merits of the case before them and accordingly determine upon peace or war. If it is the latter, before taking up arms, they send a priest called a Tribune to the enemy to demand that he give up his conquests or, as the case may be, stop his tyrannizing. If the enemy refuses, war is forthwith declared, and the God of Vengeance is invoked to bear witness against the wrongdoer. If the enemy attempts to temporize, they do not give him time. They allow a king no more than an hour to reply; they allow a republic only three hours to do so as to avoid any possibility of being fooled. If the enemy will not bow to reason, war follows. Once it is embarked upon, Power's lieutenant takes charge of everything. Power may give orders without seeking counsel of anyone, unless there is a question of great moment, in which case he will consult Love, Wisdom, or Sun. All the people, women as well as men, who are twenty years old or

71

di venti anni in su, e le donne ancora, e si dichiara la giustizia dell'impresa dal Predicatore, e metteno in ordine ogni cosa.

Devesi sapere ch'essi hanno tutte sorti de arme apparecchiate nell'armari, e spesso si provano quelle in guerre finte. Han per tutti li gironi, nell'esterior muro, l'artellerie e l'archebugi preparati e molti altri cannoni di campagna che portano in guerra, e n'han pur di legno, nonchè di metallo; e così sopra le carra li conducono, e l'altre munizioni nelli muli, e bagaglie. E se sono in campo aperto, serrano le bagaglie in mezzo e l'artellerie, e combattono gran pezzo, e poi fan la ritirata. E 'l nemico, credendo che cedano, s'inganna; perchè essi fanno ala, pigliano fiato e lasciano l'artiglierie sparare, e poi tornano all zuffa contro nemici scompigliati. Usano far i padiglioni alla romana con steccati e fosse intorno con gran prestezza. Ci son li mastri di bagaglie, d'artellerie e dell'opere. Tutti soldati san maneggiar la zappa e la secure. Vi son cinque, otto o diece capitani di consiglio di guerra e di stratagemme, che comandano alle squadre loro secondo prima insieme si consigliôrno. Soleno portar seco una squadra di fanciulli a cavallo per imparar la guerra e incarnarsi, come lupicini, al sangue; e nei pericoli si ritirano, e molte donne con loro. E dopo la battaglia esse donne e fanciulli fanno carezze alli guerrieri, li medicano, serveno, abbracciano e confortano; e quelli, per mostrarsi valenti alle donne e figli loro, fanno gran prove. Nell'assalti, chi prima saglie il muro ha dopo in onore una

more are summoned to an assembly where they hear the justice of their cause proclaimed by the Orator, and all things are put in order.

You must understand that in their armories they have all sorts of weapons in readiness which have been repeatedly tested in their military maneuvers. There are manned artillery emplacements on the outer walls of every circuit of the city. In addition they possess many field guns which they can bring into battle. These are made of wood as well as metal and can be transported on wagons while other munitions are transported by mule pack or baggage train. If they find themselves in an open field, they encircle their baggage trains and artillery, fight for a long stretch, and then retreat, thus deceiving the enemy into believing that they are quitting; but in fact they are only catching their breath and regrouping while their artillery discharges its shot. Then they resume the fight against a disorganized enemy. They are accustomed to throwing up hasty fortifications in the Roman manner with stockades and ditches. Baggage trains, artillery, and battle engines are all in the care of special officers. As to mattocks and axes, every soldier knows their use. A staff of five, eight, or ten captains are in charge of planning and strategy, and these command their squadrons to execute the orders previously determined upon. Customarily, they also have a squadron of boys, mounted on horseback, who accompany them into battle so as to learn war and to habituate themselves, like whelps, to the sight of blood. In time of danger these are ordered to withdraw, as are also the women. When the battle is over, the boys and the women comfort the warriors, provide medical aid, serve them, and embrace them. To show their worth before such eyewitnesses, the warriors display extraordinary courage. The first to scale the walls in an

73

corona di gramigna con applauso militare delle donne e fanciulli. Chi aiuta il compagno ha la corona civica di quercia; chi uccide il tiranno, le spoglie optime, che porta al tempio, e si dona dal Sole il cognome dell'impresa.

Usano i cavalieri una lancia, due pistole avanti cavallo, di mirabil tempra, strette in bocca, che per questo passano ogn'armatura, e hanno anco lo stocco. Altri portano la mazza, e questi son gli uomini d'arme, perchè, non potendo un'armatura ferrea penetrare con spada o con pistola, sempre assaltano il nemico con la mazza, come Achille contra Cigno, e lo sconquassano e gittano. Ha due catene la mazza in punta, a cui pendeno due palle, che, menando, circondano il collo del nemico, lo cingeno, tirano e gettano; e, per poterla maneggiare, non tengono briglia con mano, ma con li piedi, incrocicchiata nella sella, e avvinchiata nell'estremo alle staffe, non alli piedi, per non impedirsi; e le staffe han di fuori la sfera e dentro il triangolo, onde in piede torcendo ne' lati, le fan girare, chè stan affibiate alli staffili, e così tirano a sè o allongano il freno con mirabil prestezza, e con la destra torceno a sinistra e *a contrario*. Questo secreto manco i Tartari hanno inteso, chè stirare e torcere non sanno con le staffe. Li cavalli leggeri cominciano con li schioppi, e poi entrano l'aste e le frombole, delle quali tengono gran conto. E usano combattere per fila intessute, andando altri, e altri ritirandosi a

assault is afterwards honored with a crown of couch grass and the applause of the assembled women and boys. Anyone who helps a comrade receives a civic crown of oak leaves. The warrior who slays the tyrant receives the prize of the spoils, which he then bears to the temple, and Sun bestows the name of the campaign upon him as a surname.

The mounted warriors for the most part carry a lance, a sword, and, in their saddles, two pistols made of steel of amazing temper. These are of small calibre and for this reason can pierce the strongest armor. Other mounted troops are armed with the mace. These go heavily armored, and wherever sword or pistol cannot penetrate the armor of the enemy, they strike with the mace as Achilles did against Cygnus,[30] thereby smashing the enemy and throwing him down. The mace they use has two chains attached to the head of it, each of which carries a metal ball at the other end. Thus when the warrior swings it at an opponent, these chains clutch the opponent's neck and pull him down. In order to handle this weapon the warrior manages the reins with his feet instead of his hands, crossing the straps over the saddle and attaching the ends to the stirrups, not to the feet, for this would impede him. The stirrups have a ring outside and a triangle within, and so by turning them with his feet, he can pull or slacken the reins with great speed.[31] With the right foot, he can turn the horse to the left, and with the left foot, he can turn it to the right. This secret even the Tartars have not heard of, for they do not know how to draw in and turn by means of the stirrups. Armed with guns, the light cavalry leads the attack. Then follow the lancers and the archers, who are held in high regard. They customarily fight in a formation of interweaving lines, which are constantly replenished with fresh troops as others with-

vicenda; e hanno li squadroni saldi delle picche per fermezza del campo; e le spade sono l'ultima prova.

Ci son poi li trionfi militari ad uso di Romani, e più belli, e le supplicazioni ringraziatorie. E si presenta al tempio il capitano, e si narrano li gesti dal poeta o istorico ch'andò con lui. E 'l principe lo corona, e a tutti soldati fa qualche regalo e onore, e per molti dì sono esenti dalle fatiche publiche. Ma essi l'hanno a male, perchè non sanno star oziosi e aiutano gli altri. E all'incontro quei che per loro colpa han perduto, si ricevono con vituperio, e chi fu il primo a fuggire non può scampar la morte, se non quando tutto l'esercito domanda in grazia la sua vita, e ognun piglia parte della pena. Ma poco s'ammette tal indulgenza, si non quando ci è gran ragione. Chi non aiutò l'amico o fece atto vile, è frustato; chi fu disobediente, si mette a morire dentro un palco di bestie con un bastone in mano, e se vince i leoni e l'orsi, che è quasi impossibile, torna in grazia.

Le città superate o date a loro subito mettono ogni avere in commune, e riceveno gli offiziali solari e la guardia, e si van sempre acconciando all'uso della Città del Sole, maestra loro; e mandano li figli ad imparare in quella, senza contribuire a spese.

Saria lungo a dirti del mastro delle spie e sentinelle,

draw. For protection of the camp they have massed squadrons of pikemen. The swordsmen are the last to engage in battle.

After the battle there are military triumphs like those of the Romans, but even more impressive. Prayers of thanksgiving are offered up. The commander presents himself at the temple, and the poet or historian who accompanied the troops into battle then rehearses their deeds. The ruler crowns the commander and distributes gifts and honors among all the soldiers. For many days after, they are exempt from all public duties. But they do not take well to these exemptions, for they do not know how to remain idle; so they lend assistance to others. On the other hand, those who through some fault of their own suffered defeat in battle are afterwards disgraced, and the one among them who was the first to flee does not escape the death penalty unless the entire army pleads for his life and agrees to assume part of his punishment. But this indulgence is seldom granted except for the most persuasive reasons. Any soldier who is guilty of having failed to help his comrade or of having displayed cowardice is flogged. Anyone who has disobeyed orders is given a club and placed in an enclosure containing wild beasts. If he succeeds in overcoming the lions and bears—almost an impossibility—he is restored to favor.

The conquered cities and those surrendered to the victors immediately change over to the system of communal ownership of all goods. They receive Solarian officials and a garrison from the City of the Sun and proceed to model their institutions after those of that city, which is henceforth their guide. They also send their children to study in the City of the Sun and pay nothing for their maintenance.

It would require too long to tell you about their master of spies and of lookouts and of their organization

degli ordini loro dentro e fuore la città, che te li puoi pensare, chè son eletti da bambini secondo l'inclinazione e costellazione vista nella genitura loro. Onde ognuno, oprando secondo la proprietà sua naturale, fa bene quell'esercizio e con piacere per esserli naturale; così dico delle stratagemme e altri, ecc. La città di notte e di giorno ha le guardie nelle quattro porte e nelle mura estreme, su li torrioni e valguardi; e il giorno al più le femine, la notte li maschi guardano; e questo lo fanno per non impoltronire e per li casi fortuiti. Han le veglie, come i nostri soldati, divise di tre in tre ore; la sera entrano in guardia.

Usano le cacce per imagini di guerra, e li giochi in piazza a cavallo e a piede ogni festa, e poi segue la musica, ecc.

Perdonano volentieri a' nemici e dopo la vittoria li fanno bene. Se gettano mura o vogliono occider i capi o altro danno a' vinti, tutto fanno in un giorno, e poi li fanno bene, e dicono che non si deve far guerra se non per far gli uomini buoni, non per estinguerli. Se tra loro ci è qualche gara d'ingiuria o d'altro, perchè essi non contendono se non di onore, il Principe e suoi offiziali puniscono il reo severamente, s'incorse ad ingiuria di fatto dopo le prime ire; se di parole, aspettano in guerra a diffinirle, dicendo che l'ira si deve sfogare contro l'inimici. E chi fa poi in guerra più atti eroici, quello è tenuto c'abbia raggione nell'onoranza, e l'altro cede. Ma nelle cose del giusto ci son le pene; però in duello di mano non

both within and beyond the city. How efficient these are you can imagine for yourself, since they are selected for their tasks in infancy according to the constellation that was visible at their birth. Thus each one, working according to the inclination of his nature, does his work happily and well because it is natural to him. I am referring to both their stratagems and other matters. Night and day, guards stand posted at the four gates of the city, along the outer walls, in the towers, and on the bastions. By day the women do guard duty, by night the men. This is required to discourage indolence and as a precaution against the unexpected. They take turns in standing watch, just as our soldiers do, and are rotated every three hours beginning at sunset.

They engage in hunting as a form of mock warfare, and on holidays they have games in the city square—some played on horseback, some on foot—after which they hear music, etc.

They willingly pardon their enemies and, after defeating them, seek to be kind to them. If they must tear down enemy fortifications, slay the leaders, or do some other injury to the vanquished, they do all these things in one day.[32] Thereafter they show kindness, and they affirm that war should never be undertaken except to make men good, not to destroy them. If some conflict should arise among inhabitants of the City of the Sun as the result of insult or injury of some kind—since they never contend over anything but honors—the ruler and his officials punish the wrongdoer severely, provided he committed the wrong after his initial anger had worn off. If the injury is of a verbal nature, then the parties must withhold settlement until there is a war, since they say that anger can only be vented against a foreign host. The party to the conflict who then performs the greatest acts of heroism is considered to be in the right, and his opponent yields to him. But there are punishments in

ponno venire, e chi vol mostrarsi megliore, faccilo in guerra publica.

OSPITALARIO. Bella cosa per non fomentar fazioni a roina della patria e schifar le guerre civili, onde nasce il tiranno, come fu in Roma e Atene. Narra or, ti prego, dell'artefici loro.

GENOVESE. Devi aver inteso come commune a tutti è l'arte militare, l'agricoltura, la pastorale; ch'ognuno è obligato a saperle, e queste son le più nobili tra loro; ma chi più arti sa, più nobile è, e nell'esercitarla quello è posto, che più è atto. L'arti fatigose e utili son di più laude, come il ferraro, il fabricatore; e non si schifa nullo a pigliarle, tanto più che nella natività loro si vede l'inclinazione, e tra loro, per lo compartimento delle fatiche, nullo viene a participar fatica destruttiva dell'individuo, ma solo conservativa. L'arti che sono di manco fatica son delle femine. Le speculative son di tutti, e chi più è eccellente si fa lettore; e questo è più onorato che nelle meccaniche, e si fa sacerdote. Saper natare è a tutti necessario, e ci sono a posta le piscine fuor, nelle fosse della città, e dentro vi son le fontane.

La mercatura a loro poco serve, ma però conoscono il valor delle monete, e batteno moneta per l'ambasciatori loro, acciocchè possino commutare con la pecunia il vitto che non ponno portare, e fanno venire d'ogni parte del mondo mercanti a loro per smaltir le cose soverchie, e non vogliono danari, se non merci di quelle cose che

matters involving the law. Dueling is not allowed, however, and anyone who wishes to show himself the better man must do so in warfare.

HOSPITALER. These are wonderful things for discouraging factionalism, which is harmful to a country, and for shunning civil wars, which pave the way for the tyrant, as happened in Rome and Athens. Now I beg you to tell me about the kind of work they engage in.

GENOESE. You have already seen that military service and work in the fields and pastures are common to everyone and that everyone must be familiar with them. They regard these activities as the noblest, but they consider the noblest man to be the one who has mastered the greatest number of skills, though each individual is assigned to the work he has the greatest aptitude for. The more laborious and utilitarian tasks, like those of the blacksmith and mason, are the more praiseworthy, and no one shuns them. This is all the more true because the particular inclination of each person is seen in his birth, and in the division of labor no one is assigned to things that are destructive to his individuality but rather to things that preserve it. Tasks that are the least fatiguing are given to women. The speculative arts belong to everyone, and in each of them the person with the greatest skill is made instructor. These are more highly esteemed than the mechanical arts, and so those who teach them are designated priests. Everyone must know how to swim. For this reason pools have been excavated in the city moats, and there are fountains within.

Trade is of little use to them, but they know the value of money, and they coin it for their ambassadors, who use it to acquire the food and necessities they cannot carry with them. They also welcome merchants from all over the world as a means of getting rid of their surplus goods, for which they will not take money, prefer-

essi non hanno. E si ridono quando vedeno i fanciulli, che quelli donano tanta robba per poco argento, ma non li vecchi. Non vogliono che schiavi o forastieri infettino la città di mali costumi; però vendono quelli che pigliano in guerra, o li mettono a cavar fosse e far esercizi faticosi fuor della città, dove sempre vanno quattro squadre di soldati a guardare il territorio e quelli che lavorano, uscendo dalle quattro porte, le quali hanno le strade di mattoni fin al mare per condotta delle robbe e facilità delli forastieri. Alli quali fanno gran carezze, li donano da mangiare per tre giorni, li lavano li piedi, li fan veder la città e l'ordine loro, entrare a consiglio e a mensa. E ci son uomini deputati a guardarli, e se voglion farsi cittadini, li provano un mese nelle ville e uno nella città, e così poi risolveno, e li ricevono con certe cerimonie e giuramenti.

L'agricoltura è in gran stima: non ci è palmo di terra che non frutti. Osservano li venti e le stelle propizie, ed escono tutti in campo armati ad arare, seminare, zappare, metere, raccogliere, vindemiare, con musiche, trombe e stendardi; e ogni cosa fanno fra pochissime ore. Hanno le carra a vela, che caminano con il vento, e quando non ci è vento, una bestia tira un gran carro—bella cosa!—e han li guardiani del territorio armati, che per li campi sempre van girando. Poco usano letame all'orti e a' campi, dicendo che li semi diventano putridi e fan vita breve, come le donne imbellettate e non belle

ring instead to exchange them for goods they lack. The children, but not the adults, laugh when they see the merchants willing to give away so many things in exchange for a bit of silver. Slaves and aliens are not permitted to corrupt the manners of the city; thus those captured in war are sold, or they are put to digging ditches or performing other fatiguing tasks outside the city, where four squadrons of soldiers are regularly dispatched to supervise them and watch over the territory. These four squadrons troop out of the four city gates onto highways that are paved with stone all the way to the sea so as to expedite the movement of goods and of foreigners, whom they treat with great kindness. They wash their feet, provide them with food for three days, show them about the city, explain their ordinances to them, and allow them to attend both their council and their dining halls. There are men assigned to watch over them; and if any foreigner expressly wishes to become a citizen, he is given a probationary period of residence—one month in the country and one in the city—after which the question is decided. Before becoming a citizen, he participates in certain ceremonies and takes certain oaths.

Agriculture is held in high regard. There is not a foot of ground that is unproductive. In matters relating to this occupation the winds and propitious stars are consulted. All the people go out into the fields with banners flying, with trumpets and other instruments sounding, equipped according to the occasion, whether to hoe, plow, reap, sow, gather, or harvest. Everything is accomplished in a few hours. They have wagons that are driven by sail; and when there is no wind, one beast is enough to draw even a large one—a wonderful thing! Moreover, they have armed scouts who constantly patrol the fields. They make little use of manure, claiming that it causes seeds to rot and shortens the life of plants,

per esercizio fanno prole fiacca. Onde nè pur la terra imbellettano, ma ben l'esercitano, e hanno gran secreti di far nascer presto e multiplicare, e non perder seme. E tengon un libro a posta di tal esercizio, che si chiama la *Georgica*. Una parte del territorio, quanto basta, si ara; l'altra serve per pascolo delle bestie. Or questa nobil arte di far cavalli, bovi, pecore, cani e ogni sorte d'animali domestici è in sommo pregio appresso loro, come fu in tempo antico d'Abramo; e con modi magici li fanno venire al coito, che possan ben generare, inanzi a cavalli pinti o bovi o pecore; e non lasciano andar in campagna li stalloni con le giumente, ma li donano a tempo opportuno inanzi alle stalle di campagna. Osservano Sagittario in ascendente, con buono aspetto di Marte e Giove: per li bovi, Tauro; per le pecore, Ariete, secondo l'arte. Hanno poi mandre di galline sotto le Pleiadi e papare e anatre, guidate a pascere dalle donne con gusto loro presso alla città e li luochi dove la sera son serrate. A far il cascio e latticini, butiri e simili molto attendono, e a' caponi e a' castrati e al frutto; e ci è un libro di quest'arte detto la *Buccolica*. E abbondano d'ogni cosa, perchè ognuno desidera esser primo alla fatica per la docilità delli costumi e per esser poca e fruttuosa; e ognun di loro, che è capo di questo esercizio, s'appella re, dicendo che questo è nome loro proprio, e non di chi non sa. Gran cosa, che donne e uomini sempre vanno in squadroni, nè mai soli, e sempre all'obedienza del capo

just as women who owe their beauty to cosmetics rather than to exercise bear sickly children. Hence they will not, in a manner of speaking, apply cosmetics to the soil but prefer to work it a good deal. In addition, they are in possession of secrets that quicken and multiply growth while preventing the wasting of seeds. They have a book called the *Georgica*[33] in which these secrets are explained. Only enough ground to satisfy their needs is planted. The rest is given over to pasturage. Highly esteemed among them is the art of breeding horses, bulls, sheep, dogs, and every sort of domestic animal, just as it was in the time of Abraham. Methods employing magic are used to induce these creatures to breed in the presence of paintings of horses, bulls, or sheep.[34] They do not set stallions and mares loose in the meadows but instead bring them together outside their farm stables at the opportune time. According to their art, they wait upon Sagittarius to be in the ascendant, with Mars and Jupiter in favorable aspect, for breeding horses, upon Taurus for breeding bulls, upon Aries for breeding sheep. Under the Pleiades they keep flocks of chickens, geese, and ducks that the women herd about as they please around the city and near the enclosed places where they are kept at night. They devote a good deal of attention to making cheese, butter, and similar dairy foods; also to capons, other castrated animals, and the young.[35] A book called the *Buccolica* sets forth the practice of these arts for them. Since everyone strives to be first in his task because of his training and because the work is both short and fruitful, they abound in all things. Each person who stands at the head of his particular function is called King, for the people say that this title properly belongs to those who excel and not to those who are ignorant. It is wonderful to see that men and women always go about in squads, never alone,

si trovano senza nullo disgusto; e ciò perchè l'hanno come padre o frate maggiore.

Han poi le montagne e le cacce d'animali, e spesso s'esercitano.

La marinaria è di molta reputazione, e tengono alcuni vascelli, che senza vento e senza remi caminano, e altri con vento e remi. Intendono assai le stelle, e flussi e reflussi del mare, e navigano per conoscer genti e paesi. A nullo fan torto; senza esser stimolati non combattono. Dicono che il mondo averà da riducersi a vivere come essi fanno, però cercano sempre sapere se altri vivono meglio di loro. Hanno confederazione con li Chinesi, e con più popoli isolani e del continente di Siam e di Cancacina e Calicut, solo per spiare.

Hanno anche gran secreti di fuochi artifiziali per le guerre marine e terrestri, e stratagemme, che mai non restan di vincere.

OSPITALARIO. Che e come mangiano? e quanto è lunga la vita loro?

GENOVESE. Essi dicono che prima bisogna mirar la vita del tutto e poi delle parti; onde quando edificâro la città, posero i segni fissi nelli quattro angoli del mondo. Il Sole in ascendente in Leone, e Giove in Leone orientale dal Sole, e Mercurio e Venere in Cancro, ma vicini, che facean satellizio; Marte nella nona in Ariete, che mirava di sua casa con felice aspetto l'ascendente e l'afeta, e la Luna in Tauro, che mirava di buono aspetto Mercurio e Venere, e non facea aspetto quadrato al Sole. Stava Saturno entrando nella quarta, senza far mal aspetto a Marte e al Sole. La Fortuna con il Capo di Medusa in

and that they always willingly obey their leader without the slightest displeasure; this is because they regard him as a father or elder brother.

There are frequent hunts in the mountains, where there are many wild animals.

Navigation is also highly regarded, and they have vessels that move without wind or oar, while others are propelled by both wind and oar. They understand the stars, the ebb and flow of tides, and they travel to learn about other countries and people. To no one do they bring harm. Without provocation they will not fight. They are convinced that the whole world will eventually bring itself to live as they do. Yet they are forever exploring to learn if others live better than they do. They have treaties with the Chinese and with other people of the islands and of the continent—with Siam, Cochin-China, Calcutta—solely to explore them.

They also know great secrets about how to produce artificial fires for use in naval and land warfare and secrets of strategy by which they never fail to be victorious.

HOSPITALER. What do they eat, and how? And what is their life span?

GENOESE. They believe that first the whole of life should be examined and then its respective parts. Therefore, when they founded their city, they set the fixed signs at the four corners of the world—the sun in the ascendant in Leo; Jupiter in Leo oriental to the sun; Mercury and Venus in Cancer, but so close as to produce satellite influence; Mars in the ninth house in Aries looking out with benefic aspect upon the ascendant and the *apheta*; the moon in Taurus looking upon Mercury and Venus with benefic aspect, but not at right angles to the sun; Saturn entering the fourth house without casting a malefic aspect upon Mars and the sun;[36] Fortune with the Head of Medusa almost in the tenth house—

decima quasi era, onde essi s'augurano signoria, fermezza e grandezza. E Mercurio, sendo in buono aspetto di Vergine e nella triplicità dell'asside suo, illuminato dalla Luna, non può esser tristo; ma, sendo gioviale la scienza loro, non mendica, poco si curâro d'aspettarlo in Vergine e la congiunzione.

Or essi mangiano carne, butiri, mèle, cascio, dattili, erbe diverse, e prima non volean uccidere gli animali, parendo crudeltà; ma poi, vedendo che era pur crudeltà ammazzar l'erbe, che han senso, onde bisognava morire, considerâro che le cose ignobili son fatte per le nobili, e magnano ogni cosa. Non però uccidono volontieri l'animali fruttuosi, come bovi e cavalli. Hanno però distinti li cibi utili dalli disutili, e secondo la medicina si serveno: una fiata mangiano carne, una pesce e una erbe, e poi tornano alla carne per circolo, per non gravare nè estenuare la natura. Li vecchi han cibi più digestibili, e mangiano tre volte il giorno e poco, li fanciulli quattro, la communità due. Vivono almeno cento anni, al più centosettanta o ducento al rarissimo. E son molto temperati nel bevere: vino non si dona a' fanciulli sino alli diciannove anni senza necessità grandissima, e bevono con acqua poi, e così le donne; li vecchi di cinquanta anni in su beveno senz'acqua, ma, quando han da fare qualche consiglio o giudizio, mettono acqua. Mangiano, secondo la stagione dell'anno, quel che è più utile e proprio, secondo provisto viene dal capo Medico, che ha cura. Usano assai l'odori: la mattina,

from which circumstances they augur dominion, stability, and greatness for themselves.[37] Being in a benefic aspect of Virgo, in the triplicity of its apsis and illuminated by the moon, Mercury could not be harmful; but since their science is jovial and not beggarly, they were not concerned about Mercury's entering Virgo and the conjunction.[38]

They eat meat, butter, honey, cheese, dates, and various kinds of greens. At first they were unwilling to butcher animals because they thought it cruel to do so. But then, realizing that is was also cruel to kill plants (for they too have sense) and that they must needs starve without plants and animals for food, they concluded that the lesser creatures are made for the greater, and so they eat both. However, they will not willingly kill such work animals as oxen and horses. Using their knowledge of medicine, they distinguish between foods that are beneficial and foods that are not. On one occasion they will eat meat, on another fish, on still another greens, returning next again to meat, so that nature is neither weakened nor overburdened. To the aged go the most digestible dishes, but in rather scant portions, three times a day. Children have four meals a day, and all others have two. The life span of the people is at least a hundred years, most of them reaching a hundred and seventy and a rare few reaching two hundred years. As for drink, in this they are very moderate. Barring extremely urgent circumstances, the young are not allowed to touch wine at all until they are nineteen years of age. After that they may drink it diluted with water, as the women do. Men of fifty and over may drink it neat, but if they have to give counsel or render a decision they dilute it. They eat what is most beneficial and suitable according to season, as determined by the Chief Physician, who has charge of diet. The Solarians make great use of fragrances. When they rise in the morning,

quando si levano, si pettinano e lavano con acqua fresca tutti; poi masticano maiorana o petrosino o menta, e se la frecano nelle mani, e li vecchi usano incenso; e fanno orazione brevissima al levante come il *Pater noster*; ed escono e vanno chi a servire i vecchi, chi in coro, chi ad apparecchiare le cose del commune; e poi si riducono alle prime lezioni, poi al tempio, poi escono all'esercizio, poi riposano poco, sedendo, e vanno a magnare.

Tra loro non ci è podagre, nè chiragre, nè catarri, nè sciatiche, nè doglie coliche, nè flati, perchè questi nascono dalla distillazione e inflazione, ed essi per l'esercizio purgano ogni flato e umore. Onde è tenuto a vergogna che uno si vegga sputare, dicendo che questo nasce da poco esercizio, da poltroneria o da mangiar ingordo. Patiscono più tosto d'infiammazioni e spasmi secchi alli quali con la copia del buon cibo e bagni sovvengono; e all'etica con bagni dolci e latticini, e star in campagne amene in bello esercizio. Morbo venereo non può allignare, perchè si lavano spesso li corpi con vino e ogli aromatici; e il sudore anche leva quell'infetto vapore, che putrefà il sangue e le midolle. Nè tisici si fanno, per non esser distillazione che cali al petto, e molto meno asma, poichè umor grosso ci vuole a farla. Curano le febri ardenti con acqua fresca, e l'efimere solo con odori e brodi grassi e con dormire, o con suoni e allegrie; le terzane con levar sangue e con reubarbaro o simili attrattivi, e con bevere acque di radici d'erbe purganti e acetose. Di rado vengono a medicine purganti. Le quartane son facili a sanare per paure sùbite, per erbe

they wash themselves in fresh water, comb their hair, and then chew some marjoram, parsley, or mint and rub it on their hands. The older folks use incense. After this, everyone turns to the east and recites a short prayer similar to our *Pater noster*. Then all go out, some to join their group, some to serve the aged, some to prepare things for the commons. Later they assemble for the first lecture and then go to temple. Following this, they take part in physical exercises, sit down and rest a while, and then go to dinner.

No one among them ever suffers from gout, either of the hands or of the feet, nor from catarrhs, sciatica, colic, or flatulence since all these maladies arise from an excess of humors and from swelling which they avoid by exercising. Consequently, they consider it shameful if anyone is seen spitting, since they believe this to arise from inactivity, laziness, or gluttony. Cases of inflammation and dry spasm are more likely among them, and these they cure by bathing and by eating wholesome foods. Hectic fever they cure with sweet water baths and dairy foods accompanied by mild exercise and by rest in the country. They are not susceptible to venereal diseases because they often wash their bodies with wine and aromatic oils. Sweating is also helpful in dispelling those infectious vapors that corrupt the blood and marrow. They do not have consumption because they do not suffer from an excess of humor settling in the chest. Still less do they have asthma since this comes from a heaviness of humor. Burning fevers they cure by fresh water and mild ones by nothing more than sweet odors and fatty broth, by sleep, or by music and gaiety. Tertian fevers are treated by bloodletting, by the use of rhubarb or similar drawing agents, and by potations of juices pressed from the roots of purgative and acetic herbs. But purgative medicines are rarely needed. Quartan fevers they easily cure by subjecting the pa-

simili all'umore od opposite; e mi mostrâro certi secreti mirabili di quelle. Delle continue tengono conto assai, e fanno osservanze di stelle ed erbe, e preghiere a Dio per sanarle. Quintane, ottane, settane poche si trovano, dove non ci sono umori grossi. Usano li bagni e l'olei all'usanza antica, e ci trovâro molto più secreti per star netto, sano, gagliardo. Si forzano con questi e altri modi aiutarsi contro il morbo sacro, chè ne pateno spesso.

OSPITALARIO. Segno d'ingegno grande, onde Ercole, Socrate, Macometto, Scoto e Callimaco ne patîro.

GENOVESE. E s'aiutano con preghiere al cielo e con odori e confortamenti della testa e cose acide e allegrezze e brodi grassi, sparsi di fiore di farina. Nel condir le vivande non han pari: pongono macis, mèle, butiro e con aromati assai, che ti confortano grandemente. Non beveno annevato, come i Napolitani, neanche caldo, come li Chinesi, perchè non han bisogno d'aiutarsi contro l'umori grossi in favor del natio calore, ma lo confortano con aglio pesto e aceto, serpillo, menta, basilico, l'estate e nella stanchezza; nè contra il soverchio calor dall'aromati aumentato, perchè non escono di regola. Hanno pur un secreto di rinovar la vita ogni sette anni, senza afflizione, con bell'arte.

OSPITALARIO. Non hai ancora detto delle scienze e degli offiziali.

GENOVESE. Sì, ma poichè sei tanto curioso, ti dirò più. Ogni nova luna e ogni opposizione sua fanno consiglio dopo il sacrifizio; e qui entrano tutti di venti anni

tient to sudden frights or by administering herbs that are either similar to the disordered humor or the opposite of it. Regarding these herbs they revealed a number of secrets to me. About continual fevers they are much concerned; to cure them, they observe the stars, inspect herbs, and pray to God. Quintan, octan, and heptan fevers occur only infrequently where heavy humors are lacking. They use baths and oils as the ancients did and have discovered many secrets by which to remain clear, strong, and sound. With these and other remedies they make every effort to guard against the sacred sickness[39] from which they often suffer.

HOSPITALER. A sign of great cleverness, since Hercules, Socrates, Muhammad, Duns Scotus, and Callimachus suffered from it.

GENOESE. To guard against it, they use prayers, fragrances, head comforters, sour things, gaiety, and fatty broths sprinkled with flour. In preparing tasty dishes that are a delight they have no equals. They make great use of mace, honey, butter, and many aromatic herbs. They do not imbibe iced drinks as the Neapolitans do, nor heated ones as the Chinese do, for they are in no need of help to guard against heavy humors by abetting their natural heat. But in summer or when they are tired they spice their drink with crushed garlic and vinegar, with wild thyme, mint, and basil. Nor need they guard against the heat of the aromatics they add to their drink, for they practice moderation. However, they know a secret, marvelous art by which they can renew their bodies painlessly every seven years.

HOSPITALER. You have not yet spoken about their sciences and about their officials.

GENOESE. Indeed I have, but since you are so curious, I will tell you more. At every new moon and at every full moon, they make a sacrifice and then summon a general council to which everyone who is twenty years

in suso, e si dimanda ad ognuno che cosa manca alla città, e chi offiziale è buono e chi è tristo. Dopo ogn'otto dì, si congregano tutti l'offiziali, che son il Sole, Pon, Sin, Mor; e ognun di questi ha tre offiziali sotto di sè, che son tredici, e ognun di questi tre altri, che fan tutti quaranta; e quelli han l'offizi dell'arti convenienti a loro, il Potestà della milizia, il Sapienza delle scienze, il Amore del vitto, generazione e vestito ed educazione; e li mastri d'ogni squadra, cioè caporioni, decurioni, centurioni sì delle donne come degli uomini. E si ragiona di quel che bisogna al publico, e si eleggon gli offiziali, pria nominati in consiglio grande. Dopo ogni dì fa consiglio Sole e li tre prencipi delle cose occorrenti, e confirmano e conciano quel che si è trattato nell'elezione e gli altri bisogni. Non usano sorti, se non quando son dubbi in modo che non sanno a qual parte pendere. Questi offiziali si mutano secondo la volontà del popolo inchina, ma li quattro primi no, se non quando essi stessi, per consiglio fatto tra loro, cedono a chi veggono saper più di loro e aver più purgato ingegno; e son tanto docili e buoni, che volentieri cedeno a chi più sa e imparano da quelli; ma questo è di rado assai.

Li capi principali delle scienze son soggetti al Sapienza, altri che il Metafisico, che è esso Sole, che a tutte scienze comanda, come architetto, e ha vergogna ignorare cosa alcuna al modo umano. Sotto a lui sta il

of age or more may come. Each person present at this council is asked to tell what he thinks the city lacks, which officials he considers good and which ones bad. Every eight days the officials themselves assemble together. These are Sun, Pon, Sin, and Mor,[40] who, together with the three subordinate officials assigned to each of them, make a total of thirteen[41] and, together with the three sub-officials assigned to each of the subordinates, make a total of forty in all. Each of these men has charge over his proper sphere of activity. Power has charge of the army; Wisdom has charge of the sciences; Love has charge of food, of breeding the species, of dress, and of education. Below these leaders stand the masters of every squadron, whether composed of one hundred, fifty, or ten persons, whether men or women. Together these heads discuss the needs of the public and elect officials from among candidates nominated by the general council. At the end of each day Sun and the three chief officials consult about whatever needs to be done, approving or amending the results of the election and considering other matters as well. In choosing, they never employ lots except in doubtful cases which can be resolved in no other way. Elected officials keep their post as long as the people wish them to; but the four chief officials only leave office when they, in counsel among themselves, decide to give way to a successor whom they recognize as knowing more and having a clearer intelligence than they do. They are so modest and good that they have no reluctance about giving way to anyone who is their better and then seeking to learn from him. But this happens very infrequently.

Except for the Metaphysician, otherwise called Sun (who, as chief architect, commands all science and would be ashamed to be ignorant of anything that concerns humanity), the heads of all the sciences are subject to Wisdom. Subject to him, therefore, are the Gram-

Grammatico, il Logico, il Fisico, il Medico, il Politico, l'Economico, il Morale, l'Astronomo, l'Astrologo, il Geometra, il Cosmografo, il Musico, il Prospettivo, l'Aritmetico, il Poeta, l'Oratore, il Pittore, il Scultore. Sotto Amore sta il Genitario, l'Educatore, il Vestiario, l'Agricola, l'Armentario, il Pastore, il Cicurario, il Gran Coquinario. Sotto Potestà il Stratagemmario, il Campione, il Ferrario, l'Armario, l'Argentario, il Monetario, l'Ingegnero, Mastro spia, Mastro cavallarizzo, il Gladiatore, l'Artegliero, il Frombolario, il Giustiziero. E tutti questi han li particolari artefici soggetti.

Or qui hai da sapere che ognun è giudicato da quello dell'arte sua; talchè ogni capo dell'arte è giudice, e punisce d'esilio, di frusta, di vituperio, di non mangiar in mensa commune, di non andar in chiesa, non parlar alle donne. Ma quando occorre caso ingiurioso, l'omicidio si punisce con morte, e occhio per occhio e naso per naso si paga per la pena della pariglia, quando è caso pensato. Quando è rissa subitanea, si mitiga la sentenza, ma non dal giudice, perchè condanna subito secondo la legge, ma dalli tre prencipi. E s'appella pure al Metafisico per grazia, non per giustizia, e quello può far la grazia. Non tengono carcere, se non per qualche ribello nemico un torrione. Non si scrive processo, ma in presenza del giudice e del Potestà si dice il pro e il contra; e subito si condanna dal giudice; e poi dal Potestà, se s'appella, il sequente dì si condanna; e poi dal Sole il terzo dì

marian, the Logician, the Physical Scientist, the Physician, the Political Scientist, the Economist, the Moralist, the Astronomer, the Astrologer, the Geometer, the Cosmographer, the Musician, the Prospectivist, the Arithmetician, the Poet, the Orator, the Painter, and the Sculptor. Subject to Love are the Breeder, the Educator, the Clothier, the Agronomist, the Herder, the Pasturer, the Animal Raiser, and the Grand Chef. Subject to Power are the Strategist, the Champion, the Blacksmith, the Armorer, the Silversmith, the Coiner, the Engineer, the Chief Spy, the Master of the Horse, the Gladiator, the Artilleryman, the Slingmaster, and the Justicer. Each of these in turn has charge over all those who are engaged in his particular activity.

Now you must understand that each individual is judged by the chief of his craft. Thus the chief is also a judge who has the right to punish by banishment, by flogging, by censure, by withdrawing the right of the common mess, of attendance at church, or of conversing with women. In cases involving serious injury, however, the law of retaliation is invoked—an eye for an eye, a nose for a nose—if the injuring involved premeditation. Homicide is punished by death. In cases of unpremeditated violence, the sentence is mitigated, not by the judge, however, who must condemn according to law, but by the three princes. The condemned person may also appeal to the Metaphysician for mercy, though not for judgment,[42] and the Metaphysician may grant it. Except for a tower reserved for some rebel enemy, there are no prisons. Testimony given at trials is not written down. The accused and the accuser both present their arguments before the judge and Power. On the same day, immediately following the trial, the judge hands down his sentence. If this is appealed, Power hands down his sentence on the second day, and Sun hands down his on the third. On the other hand,

97

si condanna, o s'aggrazia dopo molti dì con consenso del popolo. E nessuno può morire, se tutto il popolo a man commune non l'uccide; chè boia non hanno, ma tutti lo lapidano o brugiano, facendo che esso si leghi la polvere per morir subito. E tutti piangono e pregano Dio, che plachi l'ira sua, dolendosi che sian venuti a resecare un membro infetto dal corpo della republica; e fanno di modo che esso stesso accetti la sentenza, e disputano con lui fin tanto che esso, convinto, dica che la merita; ma quando è caso contra la libertà o contra Dio o contra gli offiziali maggiori, senza misericordia si esequisce. Questi soli si puniscono con morte; e quel che more ha da dire tutte le cause perchè non deve morire, e li peccati degli altri e dell'offiziali, dicendo quelli meritano peggio; e se vince, lo mandano in esilio e purgano la città con preghiere e sacrifizi e ammende; ma non però travagliano li nominati.

Li falli di fragilità e d'ignoranza si puniscono solo con vitupèri, e con farlo imparare a contenersi, e quell'arte in cui peccò, o altra, e si trattano in modo, che paion l'un membro dell'altro.

Qui è da sapere, che se un peccatore, senza aspettar accusa, va da sè all'offiziali accusandosi e dimandando

the condemned man may be pardoned after many days with the consent of the people. Since there are no executioners, there can be no execution unless all the people take part in it, either by stoning or by burning the condemned man, allowing him in the latter case to have gunpowder so as to hasten his dying.[43] Afterwards all the people weep and then pray that God will allay His wrath, seeing how necessary it was for them to remove an infected limb from the body of the republic. They also try to argue with the condemned man until he comes to accept the sentence handed down against him and admits that it is merited. But when the case involves injury to the freedom of the republic, or to God, or to the highest officials, the sentence is carried out without mercy. Only a person found guilty of one of these crimes is punished with death. Before going to execution he is required to state all the reasons why he should not be killed; he must also enumerate all the sins committed by others, including officials, and show why they deserve a worse sentence then his own. If his argument proves convincing, the sentence is commuted to banishment. The city is then purged by prayers, by sacrifices, and by correction of faults, but the persons named in the condemned man's accusations are not made to suffer.

Faults committed through weakness or through ignorance are punished by censure alone. Those found guilty of the former are taught to control themselves, while those found guilty of the latter are made to master the craft in which they showed ignorance or to learn some other one. These things are done in such a way as to make the guilty party aware of his relationship to his fellows.

You must understand that if a transgressor goes to one of the officials of his own free will and accuses him-

ammenda, lo liberano dalla pena dell'occulto peccato e la commutano mentre non fu accusato.

Si guardano assai dalla calunnia per non patir la medesima pena. E perchè sempre stanno accompagnati quasi, ci vuole cinque testimoni a convincere; se non, si libera col giuramento il reo. Ma se due altre volte è accusato da dui o tre testimoni, al doppio paga la pena.

Le leggi son pochissime, tutte scritte in una tavola di rame alla porta del tempio, cioè nelle colonne, nelle quali ci son scritte tutte le quiddità delle cose in breve: che cosa è Dio, che cosa è angelo, che cosa è mondo, stella, uomo, ecc., con gran sale, e d'ogni virtù la diffinizione. E li giudici d'ogni virtù hanno la sedia in quel luoco, quando giudicano, e dicono: —Ecco, tu peccasti contra questa diffinizione: leggi—; e così poi lo condanna o d'ingratitudine o di pigrizia o d'ignoranza; e le condanne son certe vere medicine, più che pene, e di soavità grande.

OSPITALARIO. Or dire ti bisogna delli sacerdoti e sacrifizi e credenza loro.

GENOVESE. Sommo sacerdote è Sole; e tutti gli offiziali son sacerdoti, parlando delli capi, e offizio loro è purgar le conscienze. Talchè tutti si confessano a quelli, ed essi imparano che sorti di peccati regnano. E si confessano alli tre maggiori tanto li peccati proprii, quanto li strani in genere, senza nominare li peccatori, e li tre poi si confessano al Sole. Il quale conosce che sorti di errori corrono e sovviene alli bisogni della città e fa a Dio sacrifizio e orazioni, a cui esso confessa li peccati

self and demands punishment before anyone has accused him, he is absolved of guilt since no one else has brought charges against him.

The people are particularly careful to avoid spreading slander in order to avoid becoming victims of the same themselves. Because they are almost invariably in company and seldom alone, five witnesses are required to establish a case against a person; otherwise his own word is enough to set him free. But if the same person is accused on two further occasions by no more than two or three witnesses, his punishment is doubled.

The laws are very few, all of them being inscribed on a copper plaque placed on a column at the temple door, on which the definitions of all things are briefly set down—what God is, what an angel is, what the world, the stars, man, etc.—these are all set down with great wisdom, as are also all the virtues. And it is here that the judge of each virtue presides and renders decisions, saying, "Observe, you sinned against this definition. Read it!" Thus they sentence those who are guilty of ingratitude, of sloth, or of ignorance. And such sentences, more than any punishment, are sure correctives, powerfully beneficial.

HOSPITALER. Now you must tell me about their priests, their worship, and their beliefs.

GENOESE. Their high priest is Sun, but all the chief officials are also priests, and it is their task to purge consciences. The people make their confessions to them, and thus they learn what sins are most commonly being committed. They in turn confess both their own sins and those of others, but without naming anyone, to the three chief officials, and these make confession to Sun. Having learned what sins are being committed, Sun then provides the remedies the city requires. He offers sacrifices and prayers to God. Without singling out individuals, he confesses his own sins and those of all the

suoi e di tutto il popolo publicamente in su l'altare, ogni volta che sia necessario per amendarli, senza nominar alcuno. E così assolve il popolo, ammonendo che si guardi di quelli errori, e confessa i suoi in publico e poi fa sacrifizio a Dio, che voglia assolvere tutta la città e ammaestrarla e difenderla. Il sacrifizio è questo, che dimanda al popolo chi si vol sacrificare per li suoi membri, e così un di quelli più buoni si sacrifica. E 'l sacerdote lo pone sopra una tavola, che è tenuta da quattro funi, che stanno a quattro girelle della cupola, e, fatta l'orazione a Dio che riceva quel sacrifizio nobile e voluntario umano (non di bestie involuntarie, come fanno i Gentili), fa tirar le funi; e quello saglie in alto alla cupoletta e qui se mette in orazione; e li si dà da magnare parcamente, sino a tanto che la città è espiata. Ed esso con orazioni e digiuni prega Dio, che riceva il pronto sacrifizio suo; e così, dopo venti o trenta giorni, placata l'ira di Dio, torna a basso per le parti di fuore o si fa sacerdote; e questo è sempre onorato e ben voluto, perchè esso si dà per morto, ma Dio non vuol che mora.

Di più vi stanno ventiquattro sacerdoti sopra il tempio, li quali a mezzanotte, a mezzodì, la mattina e la sera cantano alcuni salmi a Dio; e l'offizio loro è di guardar le stelle e notare con astrolabi tutti li movimenti loro e gli effetti che producono, onde sanno in che paese che mutazione è stata e ha da essere. E questi dicono l'ore della generazione e li giorni del seminare e raccogliere, e serveno come mezzani tra Dio e gli uomini; e di essi per lo più si fanno li Soli e scriveno gran cose e investigano scienze. Non vengono a basso, se non per mangiare;

people publicly before the altar whenever it is necessary to make amends. Thus he absolves the people, warning them meanwhile to guard against their errors; he confesses his own sins publicly and then offers a sacrifice to God so that He may absolve, instruct, and defend the city. Now the sacrifice is this: Sun asks the people who among them is willing to offer himself as a sacrifice for the sake of his fellows. Someone of more than usual goodness having been accepted, he is placed upon a table supported by four ropes which run through pulleys attached to the temple dome. Prayers are then offered up that God will receive the voluntary sacrifice of a noble human being (not the involuntary sacrifice of a beast after the manner of the heathens). The ropes are then taken in, and the willing victim is raised to the dome where he prays and fasts until the city is purged. He fasts and prays that God will accept him as a ready sacrifice. After twenty or thirty days, God's wrath having been appeased, he is brought down outside the temple. He may then become a priest. But in any case he is always loved and honored thereafter by all the people because he offered to die for them, but God did not wish his death.

Twenty-four priests are stationed high in the temple to sing certain psalms in praise of God in the morning and evening, at midnight and noon. Their task is to gaze at the stars and, using astrolabes, note all their movements and the effects these produce. In this manner, they learn what changes have taken place or are to take place in every country. They establish the hour in which conception should take place, the day on which sowing and harvesting should be done, and, in general, serve as mediators between God and man. It is usually from among these priests that future Suns are chosen. They write down things of great importance and conduct scientific investigations. They never descend to

con donne non si impacciano, se non qualche volta per medicina del corpo. Va ogni dì Sole in alto e parla con loro di quel che hanno investigato sopra il benefizio della città e di tutte le nazioni del mondo. In tempio da basso sempre ha da esser uno che faccia orazione a Dio, e ogni ora si muta, come noi facciamo le quarant'ore, e questo si dice continuo sacrifizio.

Dopo mangiare si rendon grazie a Dio con musica, e poi si cantano gesti di eroi cristiani, ebrei, gentili, di tutte nazioni, per spasso e per godere. Si cantano inni d'amore e di sapienza e d'ogni virtù. Si piglia ognuno quella che più ama, e fanno alcuni balli sotto li chiostri, bellissimi. Le donne portano li capelli lunghi, inghirlandati e uniti in un groppo in mezzo la testa con una treccia. Gli uomini solo un cerro, un velo e berrettino. Usano cappelli in campagna, in casa berrette bianche o rosse o varie, secondo l'offizio e arte che fanno, e gli offiziali più grandi e pompose.

Tutte le feste loro son quattro principali, cioè quando entra il sole in Ariete, in Cancro, in Libra, in Capricorno; e fanno gran rappresentazioni belle e dotte; e ogni congiunzione e opposizione di luna fanno certe feste. E nelli giorni che fondâro la città e quando ebbero vittoria, fanno il medesimo con musica di voci femminine e con trombe e tamburi e artiglierie; e li poeti cantano le laudi delli più virtuosi. Ma chi dice bugia in laude è punito; non si può dir poeta chi finge menzogne tra loro; e questa licenza dicono che è ruina del mondo, che toglie il premio alle virtù e lo dona altrui per paura o adulazione.

the ground except to eat, and they do not bother with women except very infrequently for the health of their bodies. Every day Sun goes up to talk with them about any of their investigations that bear on the welfare of the city and of other nations of the world. Below in the temple there is always a priest offering prayers to God. Every hour he is replaced by another, as we do ours during the Forty Hours' Devotion. This they call the continuous service.[44]

After dinner, the people give thanks to God with music, and then, for both pastime and pleasure, they sing about the deeds of the Christian, Hebrew, and Gentile heroes of every nation. They also sing hymns in praise of love and wisdom and every virtue. Every man then chooses the woman he loves most and dances with her in the beautiful cloisters. The women wear their hair long and twist it into a bun on the top of their heads. The men wear theirs in a single tuft with a net and a cap. They wear hats in the fields and caps indoors that are white, red, or varicolored, according to the craft they follow. The officials wear larger, more impressive ones than the rest.

Their major festivals are four, occurring when the sun enters Aries, Cancer, Libra, and Capricorn.[45] On these occasions they present plays and shows that are both learned and beautiful. Other festivities take place at every full and every new moon. The anniversary of the city's founding and the anniversaries of their victories they celebrate with music; the women sing, drums and bugles are played, the artillery is fired in salute, and the poets sing the praises of their most virtuous citizens. But those who spice their praise with falsehoods are punished, since weavers of lies cannot be called poets, and the people say that such license is the ruin of the world because it takes the prize from virtue and bestows it elsewhere out of fear or flattery.

Non si fa statua a nullo, se non dopo che more; ma, vivendo, si scrive nel libro delli eroi chi ha trovato arti nove e secreti d'importanza, o fatto gran benefizio in guerra o pace al publico.

Non si atterrano li corpi morti, ma si bruggiano per levar la peste e per convertirsi in fuoco, cosa tanto nobile e viva, che vien dal sole e a lui torna, e per non restar sospetto d'idolatria. Restano pitture solo o statue di grand'uomini, e quelle mirano le donne formose, che s'applicano all'uso della razza.

L'orazioni si fan alli quattro angoli del mondo orizzontali, e la mattina prima a levante, poi a ponente, poi a mezzodì, poi a settentrione; la sera al riverso, prima a ponente, poi a levante, poi a settentrione, poi ad ostro. E replicano solo un verso, che dimanda corpo sano e mente sana a loro e a tutte le genti, e beatitudine, e conclude: « come par meglio a Dio ». Ma l'orazione attentamente e lunga si fa in cielo; però l'altare è tondo e in croce spartito, per dove entra Sole dopo le quattro repetizioni, e prega mirando in suso. Questo lo fan per gran misterio. Le vesti pontificali son stupende di bellezza e di significato a guisa di quelle di Aron.

Distingueno li tempi secondo l'anno tropico, non sidereo, ma sempre notano quanto anticipa questo di tempo. Credono che il sole sempre cali a basso, e però facendo più stretti circoli arriva alli tropici ed equinozi prima che l'anno passato; o vero pare arrivare, chè l'oc-

No statue is ever raised to a man until he is dead. While he is living, however, his name may be inscribed in the book of heroes—those who have revealed new arts and important secrets or have done great deeds for the people in peace or war.

The bodies of the dead are not interred, but are burned so as to avoid the risk of plague and at the same time convert them into fire, a thing so noble and lively that comes from the sun and returns to it. In this manner also every suspicion of idolatry is avoided.[46] Only the pictures and statues of great men survive, and these the shapely women devoted to the perpetuation of the race gaze upon to improve their offspring.

In saying prayers, the supplicants face the horizon at one of the four points of the compass. In the morning they first face east, then west, then south, then north. In the evening they do the reverse, first facing west, then east, then north, and lastly south. They repeat but one verse of their prayer. This contains a request for soundness of body and mind and for happiness both for themselves and for all the people, and it concludes with the phrase "as seems best to God." But the longest and most intense prayer is directed to the sky. For this reason the altar is shaped like a ring with four openings at right angles to each other. After each of his prayers to the four points of the compass, Sun goes to the center of the altar by way of these openings and prays looking upward.[47] This rite contains a great mystery for them. The pontifical robes, fashioned after those of Aaron, are extraordinarily beautiful and full of meaning.[48]

They measure time according to the tropical year, not the sidereal year, but they always observe by how much the former precedes the latter.[49] They believe that the sun is constantly coming nearer and that, by making smaller annual circuits, it arrives in the tropics and in the equinoxes earlier than the year before, or so it seems; for

chio, vedendolo più basso in obliquo, lo vede prima giungere e obliquare. Misurano li mesi con la luna e l'anno col sole; e però non accordano questo con quella fino alli dicinove anni, quando pur il Capo del drago finisce il suo corso; del che han fatto nova astronomia. Laudano Tolomeo e ammirano Copernico, benchè Aristarco e Filolao prima di lui; ma dicono che l'uno fa il conto con le pietre, l'altro con le fave, ma nullo con le stesse cose contate, e pagano il mondo con li scudi di conto, non d'oro. Però essi cercano assai sottilmente questo negozio, perchè importa a saper la fabrica del mondo, e se perirà e quando, e la sostanza delle stelle e chi ci sta dentro a loro. E credeno esser vero quel che disse Cristo delli segni delle stelle, sole e luna, li quali alli stolti non pareno veri, ma li venirà, come ladro di notte, il fin delle cose. Onde aspettano la renovazione del secolo, e forsi il fine. Dicono che è gran dubio sapere se 'l mondo fu fatto di nulla o delle rovine d'altri mondi o del caos; ma par verisimile che sia fatto, anzi certo. Son nemici d'Aristotile, l'appellano pedante.

Onorano il sole e le stelle come cose viventi e statue di Dio e tempii celesti; ma non l'adorano, e più onorano il sole. Nulla creatura adorano di latria, altro che Dio, e però a lui serveno solo sotto l'insegna del sole, ch'è insegna e volto di Dio, da cui viene la luce e 'l calore e ogni altra cosa. Però l'altare è come un sole fatto, e li sacerdoti pregano Dio nel sole e nelle stelle, com'in altari, e

the eye, seeing it nearer on the oblique, sees it arrive sooner than it actually has and sees it incline. They measure the months by the moon and the years by the sun, but they do not bring the two into accord except every nineteen years, when the Head of the Dragon has completed its course.[50] Out of this they have formed a new astronomy. They praise Ptolemy, and they admire Copernicus (though they put Aristarchus and Philolaus before him).[51] Yet they say that the one does his counting with pebbles and the other with broad beans, and neither of them uses the very things being counted. Consequently, they pay the world off with play money instead of gold.[52] However, these people are very interested in matters of this kind and study them very closely, for it is important to know how the world is constructed, whether it will end and, if so, when; what the stars are made of, and who inhabits them. They believe that what Christ said about the signs from the stars, the sun, and the moon is true,[53] though fools deny it; but the end of things will come upon them like a thief in the night.[54] Therefore these people await the renewal of the world and perhaps its end. They claim that it is difficult to determine whether the world was created out of nothing or out of the wreck of other worlds or out of chaos; but they believe it likely—indeed, certain—that it was created. They are enemies of Aristotle and call him a pedant.

They honor the sun and the stars as living things, as images of God, and as celestial temples; but they do not worship them, though they honor the sun above the rest. No creature but God do they deem worthy of *latria*,[55] and Him they serve under the sign of the sun which is the symbol and visage of God from Whom comes light and warmth and every other thing. For this reason their altar is shaped like a sun, and their priests pray to God in the sun and in the stars as though these

nel cielo, come tempio; e chiamano gli angeli buoni per intercessori, che stanno nelle stelle, vive case loro, e che le bellezze sue Dio più le mostrò in cielo e nel sole, come suo trofeo e statua.

Negano gli eccentrici ed epicicli di Tolomeo e di Copernico; affermano che sia un solo cielo, e che li pianeti da sè si movano e alzino, quando al sole si congiungeno per la luce maggiore che riceveno; e abbassino nelle quadrature e nell'opposizioni per avvicinarsi a lui. E la luna in congiunzione e opposizione s'alza per stare sotto il sole e ricever luce in questi siti assai, che la sublima. E per questo le stelle, benchè vadano sempre di levante a ponente, nell'alzare paion gir a dietro; e così si veggono, perchè il stellato cielo corre velocemente in ventiquattro ore, ed esse, ogni dì caminando meno, restano più a dietro; talchè, sendo passate dal cielo, paion tornare. E quando son nell'opposto del sole, piglian breve circolo per la bassezza, chè s'inchinano a pigliar luce da lui, e però caminano inante assai; e quando vanno a par delle stelle fisse, si dicon stazionari; quando più veloci, retrogradi, secondo li volgari astrologi; e quando meno, diretti. Ma la luna, tardissima in congiunzione e opposizione, non par tornare, ma solo avanzare inanti poco, perchè il primo cielo non è tanto più di lei veloce allora c'ha lume assai o di sopra o di sotto, onde non par retrograda, ma solo tarda indietro e veloce inanti. E così si

were His altars, and they pray to Him in the sky as though that were His temple. They say that angels, who dwell in the stars which are their living abodes, are reliable intercessors, and they declare that God most clearly revealed His beauty in the sky and in the sun, His trophy and His image.

They reject the eccentrics and epicycles of Ptolemy and Copernicus[56] and affirm that there is only one heaven and that the planets move away from us and rise by themselves when they are in conjunction with the sun because of the greater light they receive from it; they descend and come nearer to us when they are in quadrature or in opposition to the sun so that they can at the same time get nearer to it. The moon, either in conjunction or opposition, moves away from us so as to be nearer the sun and receive more light in these positions.[57] And for this reason the stars,[58] though they always move from east to west, seem at their apogee to be going backwards; so, indeed, are they seen to do[59] because the heaven of the fixed stars runs its swift course in twenty-four hours, while these, moving less rapidly and remaining progressively farther behind, at a certain point seem to reverse their course. When they are opposite the sun, they take up a lesser orbit nearer the earth so as to receive more of the sun's light, and therefore they travel more rapidly. When they keep pace with the fixed stars, they are said to be stationary; when they are faster, the common astrologers say they are retrograde; when they are slower, they are said to be direct. But the moon, being very slow when it is in conjunction and opposition, does not seem to reverse course but merely to advance slightly, because the fixed stars do not move much more rapidly that it does when it has a great deal of light behind or before it; therefore it does not seem retrograde but merely slow as it holds back and rapid as it moves ahead. Thus it is evident that neither epicycles

vede che nè epicicli, nè eccentrici ci voleno a farli alzare e retrocedere. Vero è ch'in alcune parti del mondo han consenso con le cose sopracelesti, e si fermano, e però diconsi alzar in eccentrico.

Del sole poi rendono la causa fisica, che nel settentrione s'alza per contrastar la terra, dove essa prese forza, mentre esso scorse nel merigge, quando fu il principio del mondo. Talchè in settembre bisogna dire che sia stato fatto il mondo, come gli Ebrei e Caldei antiqui, non li moderni, escogitâro: e così, alzando per rifar il suo, sta più giorni in settentrione che in austro, e par salir in eccentrico, ecc.

Tengono dui princìpi fisici: il sole padre e la terra madre; e l'aere essere cielo impuro, e 'l fuoco venir dal sole, e 'l mar essere sudore della terra liquefatta dal sole e unir l'aere con la terra, come il sangue lo spirito col corpo umano; e 'l mondo essere animal grande, e noi star intra lui, come i vermi nel nostro corpo; e però noi appartenemo alla providenza di Dio, e non del mondo e delle stelle, perchè rispetto a loro siamo casuali; ma rispetto a Dio, di cui essi sono stromenti, siamo antevisti e provisti; però a Dio solo avemo l'obligo di signore, di padre e di tutto.

Tengono per cosa certa l'immortalità dell'anima, e che s'accompagni, morendo, con spiriti buoni o rei, secondo il merito. Ma li luoghi delle pene e premi non l'han per tanto certi; ma assai ragionevole pare che sia il cielo e i luochi sotterranei. Stanno anche molto curiosi di sapere se queste pene sono eterne o no. Di più son certi che vi siano angeli buoni e tristi, come avviene tra

nor eccentrics are needed to explain the movement of stars away from or toward the earth. It is true that in certain parts of the cosmos the planets have an affinity with supercelestial things and therefore pause, and that is why it is said that they move outward on an eccentric.

Employing a physical explanation, the Solarians say that the sun rises in the northern hemisphere to oppose the earth, which first took vigor there after the creation, while the sun was in the southern hemisphere. Hence the creation must be said to have occurred in September,[60] as the ancient Hebrews and Chaldeans, but not the moderns, have explained. Rising to make good its loss, then, the sun spends more days in the northern hemisphere than in the southern, and it seems to follow an eccentric path, etc.

They believe in two physical principles: that of the sun as father and of the earth as mother. The air is impure sky; fire comes from the sun; the sea is the sweat of the earth, liquified by the sun and uniting earth and air, as blood unites the human body and spirit. The earth is a great beast and we live within it as worms live within us. As a consequence we stand under the providence of God and not that of the world and of the stars because, with respect to these, we exist by chance; but with respect to God, Whose intruments they are, we are foreknown and foreordained. Hence we are under obligation to Him alone as Lord, Father, and all.

They hold the soul's immortality a certainty and assert that after death it joins the company of good or evil spirits according to its merit. But they are not so sure about the place of reward and punishment, though it seems reasonable to them that the one must be in the sky and that the other must be underground. They are also very curious to know whether or not punishment is everlasting. In addition, they are certain that there are good and bad angels, just as there are good and bad

gli uomini, ma quel che sarà di loro aspettano avviso dal cielo. Stanno in dubbio se ci siano altri mondi fuori di questo, ma stimano pazzia dir che non ci sia niente, perchè il niente nè dentro nè fuori del mondo è, e Dio, infinito ente, non comporta il niente seco.

Fanno metafisici princìpi delle cose l'ente, ch'è Dio, e 'l niente, ch'è il mancamento d'essere, come condizione senza cui nulla si fa, perchè non se faria si fosse: dunque non era quel che si fa. Dal correre al niente nasce il male e 'l peccato; però il peccatore si dice annichilarsi e il peccato ha causa deficiente, non efficiente. La deficienza è il medesimo che mancanza, cioè o di potere o di sapere o di volere, e in questo ultimo mettono il peccato. Perchè chi può e sa ben fare, deve volere, perchè la volontà nasce da loro, ma non e contra. Qui ti stupisci ch'adorano Dio in Trinitate, dicendo ch'è somma Possanza, da cui procede somma Sapienza, e d'essi entrambi, sommo Amore. Ma non conosceno le persone distinte e nominate al modo nostro, perchè non ebbero revelazione, ma sanno ch'in Dio ci è processione e relazione di sè a sè; e così tutte cose compongono di possanza, sapienza e amore, in quanto han l'essere; d'impotenza, insipienza e disamore, in quanto pendeno dal non essere. E per quelle meritano, per queste peccano, o di peccato di natura nelli primi o d'arte in tutti tre. E così la natura par-

men, but as to what will happen to them they await word from heaven. They are uncertain whether there are other worlds beyond this one, but they think it folly to say that there is nothing beyond it, for there cannot be nothing either within or beyond the world, and nothingness is not compatible with God, Who is infinite being.

Their metaphysical principles are being, which is God, and nothingness, which is absence of being, the condition without which a thing cannot come into existence; for a thing cannot come into existence if it already exists and, therefore, that which has come into existence at some point did not exist. Evil and sin derive from our moving in the direction of non-being; that is why it is said that a sinner annihilates himself and that sin is a deficient, instead of an efficient, cause.[61] Deficiency is a lack either of power or of wisdom or of will, and it is to the last of these that they attribute sin. He who has the power and the wisdom to do good must will to do it, for will comes from the first two and not the reverse.[62] It will surprise you to know that they worship God in the Trinity, saying that God is supreme Power, whence proceeds supreme Wisdom, and that from these two comes supreme Love. But they do not distinguish and name the three persons as we do because they are not in possession of revelation. They do know, however, that in God there is procession and relation as between Self and Self; and therefore they believe that all things are composed of power, wisdom, and love insofar as they have being, and are composed of impotence, ignorance, and lack of love insofar as they incline toward non-being. By means of the first three of these, men gain merit; by means of the last three, they sin, committing sins of nature either through impotence or through ignorance or sins of intention through all three of them. Thus particular na-

ticolare pecca nel far i mostri per impotenza o ignoranza. Ma tutte queste cose son intese da Dio potentissimo, sapientissimo e ottimo, onde in lui nullo ente pecca e fuor di lui sì; ma non si va fuor di lui, se non per noi, non per lui, perchè in noi la deficienza è, in lui l'efficienza. Onde il peccare è atto di Dio, in quanto ha essere ed efficienza; ma in quanto ha non essere e deficienza, nel che consiste la quidità d'esso peccare, è in noi, ch'al non essere e disordine declinamo.

OSPITALARIO. Oh, come sono arguti!

GENOVESE. S'io avesse tenuto a mente, e non avesse pressa e paura, io ti sfondacaria gran cose; ma perdo la nave, se non mi parto.

OSPITALARIO. Per tua fè, dimmi questo solo: che dicono del peccato d'Adamo?

GENOVESE. Essi confessano che nel mondo ci sia gran corruttela, e che gli uomini si reggono follemente e non con ragione; e che i buoni pateno e i tristi reggono; benchè chiamano infelicità quella loro, perchè è annichilarsi il mostrarsi quel che non sei, cioè d'essere re, d'essere buono, d'esser savio, ecc., e non esser in verità. Dal che argomentano che ci sia stato gran scompiglio nelle cose umane, e stavano per dire con Platone, che li cieli prima giravano dall'occaso, là dove mo è il levante, e poi variâro. Dissero anco che può essere che governi qualche inferior virtù, e la Prima lo permetta, ma questa pur stimâro pazzia. Più pazzia è dire che prima resse Saturno bene, e poi Giove, e poi gli altri pianeti; ma confessano che l'età del mondo succedono secondo l'or-

ture itself sins through impotence or ignorance in creating monsters. But all these things are understood by God who is all powerful, all wise, and all good; hence no being sins in Him but only from Him. We do not turn from Him by reason of Him, however, but only by reason of ourselves, because deficiency is in us while efficiency is in Him. Hence a sin is an act of God insofar as it has being and efficiency, but insofar as it has non-being and deficiency—which constitutes the quiddity of sin—the fault is our own because we incline toward non-being and deficiency.

HOSPITALER. Oh, how subtle they are!

GENOESE. If I could remember them, if I were not in a hurry and afraid, I would reveal great things to you, but I shall miss my ship if I don't leave.

HOSPITALER. In good faith, only tell me this: what do they say about Adam's sin?

GENOESE. They admit that there is great corruption in the world and that men govern themselves foolishly, not according to reason. They say that the good suffer while the wicked rule, though such rulers are not truly happy because there is self-annihilation in pretending to be what you are not—that is, in pretending to be a king, a good and wise man, when you are not so in fact. From this they conclude that a great confusion must have entered into human affairs, and they were almost inclined to agree with Plato where he says that the heavens formerly traveled from west to east and then reversed direction.[63] They also thought it possible that some inferior virtue rules and that the Primal Virtue allows it, but now they deem it madness to believe it. Still greater madness is it to say that Saturn ruled well at the beginning and that Jupiter and the other planets followed, but they admit that the ages of the world succeed one another according to the order of the planets, and they

117

dine di pianeti, e credeno che la mutanza degli assidi ogni mille anni o mille seicento variano il mondo. E questa nostra età par che sia di Mercurio, si bene le congiunzioni magne l'intravariano, e l'anomalie han gran forza fatale.

Finalmente dicono ch'è felice il cristiano, che si contenta di credere che sia avvenuto per il peccato d'Adamo tanto scompiglio, e credeno che dai padri a' figli corre il male più della pena che della colpa. Ma dai figli al padre torna la colpa, perchè trascurâro la generazione, la fecero fuor di tempo e luoco, e in peccato, e senza scelta di genitori, e trascurâro l'educazione, chè mal l'indottrinâro. Però essi attendeno assai a questi dui punti, generazione ed educazione; e dicono che la pena e la colpa redonda alla città, tanto de' figli, quanto de' padri; però non si vedeno bene e par che il mondo si regga a caso. Ma chi mira la costruzione del mondo, l'anatomia dell'uomo (come essi fan de' condennati a morte, anatomizzandoli) e delle bestie e delle piante, e gli usi delle parti e particelle loro, è forzato a confessare la providenza di Dio ad alta voce. Però si deve l'uomo molto dedicare alla vera religione, e onorar l'autor suo; e questo non può ben fare chi non investiga l'opere sue e non attende a ben filosofare, e chi non osserva le sue leggi sante: «Quel che non vuoi per te non far ad altri, e quel che vuoi per te fa tu il medesimo.» Dal che ne segue, che se dai figli e dalle genti noi onor cercamo, alli

believe that changes in the apsides every thousand years or every thousand six hundred years produce great changes in the world.[64] They also believe that our own age seems to be under the influence of Mercury, though the superior conjunctions introduce variations and though anomalies have great determinant power.[65]

Finally they say that he is a happy Christian who is content to believe that so much disorder came about through Adam's sin, and they believe that the sins of the father are visited upon the children rather more as suffering than as blame.[66] On the other hand, the sins of the children are blamed on the parents, whether because they were negligent about conception with respect to time and place, because they allowed it to happen in sin and without concern for proper parentage, or because they neglected the children's education and training. Consequently, the Solarians attach great importance to these matters, namely breeding and education. They say that suffering and sin, both those of the father and those of the children, recoil upon the city, but because this fact is not sufficiently apparent, the world seems to be ruled by chance. However, anyone who examines the structure of the world, the anatomies of men (as these people examine the anatomies of those condemned to execution), the anatomies of animals and plants, and the function of every least organ must feel compelled loudly to proclaim the providence of God. Consequently, a man must attend to true religion with deep dedication, and he must honor his maker. No one can do this unless he investigates God's works, attends to sound philosophy, and observes his holy laws: "What you would not have done unto you do not do unto others, and what you would have done unto you, do you it likewise."[67] From this it follows that if we look for respect from our children and from others, to

quali poco damo, assai più dovemo noi a Dio, da cui tutto ricevemo, in tutto siamo e per tutto. Sia sempre lodato.

OSPITALARIO. Se questi, che seguon solo la legge della natura, sono tanto vicini al cristianesmo, che nulla cosa aggiunge alla legge naturale si non i sacramenti, io cavo argumento da questa relazione che la vera legge è la cristiana, e che, tolti gli abusi, sarà signora del mondo. E che però gli Spagnuoli trovâro il resto del mondo, benché il primo trovatore fu il Colombo vostro genovese, per unirlo tutto ad una legge; e questi filosofi saran testimoni della verità, eletti da Dio. E credo che noi non sappiamo quel che ci facemo, ma siamo instrumenti di Dio. Quelli vanno per avarizia di danari cercando novi paesi, ma Dio intende più alto fine. Il sole cerca strugger la terra, non far piante e uomini; ma Dio si serve di loro in questo. Sia laudato.

GENOVESE. Oh, se sapessi che cosa dicono per astrologia e per l'istessi profeti nostri ed ebrei e d'altre genti di questo secolo nostro, c'ha più istoria in cento anni che non ebbe il mondo in quattro mila; e più libri si fecero in questi cento che in cinque mila; e dell'invenzioni stupende della calamita e stampe e archibugi, gran segni dell'union del mondo; e come, stando nella triplicità quarta l'asside di Mercurio a tempo che le congiunzioni magne si faceano in Cancro, fece queste cose inventare per la Luna e Marte, che in quel segno valeno al navigar novo, novi regni e nove armi. Ma entrando l'asside di

whom we give little, we must show far more respect to God in whom we have our being, from whom we receive everything. May He ever be praised.

HOSPITALER. If these people who follow only the law of nature are so near to Christianity, which adds nothing but the sacraments to the law of nature, I conclude from your report that Christianity is the true law and that, once its abuses have been corrected, it will become mistress of the world. I also conclude that for this reason the Spaniards discovered the rest of the world so as to unite it all under one law, even though Columbus, your fellow Genoese, was its first discoverer. These philosophers you speak of must be elected by God to be witnesses for the truth. I see, moreover, that we know not what we do but are instruments of God. Thanks to their hunger for gold, the Spaniards go about discovering new countries, but God has a higher end in mind. The sun seeks to destroy the earth and not to create men and plants; yet God employs both sun and earth to that end. May He be praised.

GENOESE. Oh, if you only knew what they deduce from astrology and from the prophets—our own as well as the Hebrews' and those of other people—about our present century, which has produced more history in a hundred years than the whole world did in the preceding four thousand![68] More books have been written in the last century than in the previous five thousand years. And what they say about our stupendous inventions—the compass, the printing press, the harquebus—mighty signs of the imminent union of the world; and how they say that it was the apsis of Mercury, being in the fourth triplicity when the superior conjunctions were occurring in Cancer,[69] that caused these things to be invented through the influence of the moon and Mars, which, in that sign, promote new voyages, new kingdoms, and new arms. But when the apsis of Saturn

Saturno in Capricorno, e di Mercurio in Sagittario, e di Marte in Vergine, e le congiunzioni magne tornando alla triplicità prima dopo l'apparizion della stella nova in Cassiopea, sarà grande monarchia nova, e di leggi riforma e di arti, e profeti, e rinovazione. E dicono che a' Cristiani questo apporterà grand'utile; ma prima si svelle e monda, poi s'edifica e pianta.

Abbi pazienza, che ho da fare.

Questo sappi, c'han trovato l'arte del volare, che sola manca al mondo, e aspettano un occhiale di veder le stelle occulte e un oricchiale d'udir l'armonia delli moti di pianeti.

OSPITALARIO. Oh! oh! oh! mi piace. Ma Cancro è segno feminile di Venere e di Luna, e che può far di bene?

GENOVESE. Essi dicono che la femina apporta fecondità di cose in cielo, e virtù manco gagliarda rispetto a noi aver dominio. Onde si vede che in questo secolo regnano le donne, come l'Amazzoni tra la Nubbia e 'l Monopotapa, e tra gli Europei la Rossa in Turchia, la Bona in Polonia, Maria in Ongheria, Elisabetta in Inghilterra, Catarina in Francia, Margherita in Fiandra, la Bianca in Toscana, Maria in Scozia, Camilla in Roma e Isabella in Spagna, inventrice del Mondo Novo. E 'l poeta di questo secolo incominciò dalle donne dicendo:

Le donne, i cavalier, l'armi e l'amori.

E tutti son maledici li poeti d'ogge per Marte; e per Venere e per la Luna parlano di bardascismo e puttanesmo. E gli uomini si effeminano e si chiamano «Vossignoria»; e in Africa, dove regna Cancro, oltre l'Amazzoni,

enters Capricorn, when that of Mercury enters Sagittarius and that of Mars enters Virgo, and when the superior conjunctions return to the first triplicity after the appearance of the new star in Cassiopeia, there will be a great new monarchy, reformation of laws and of arts, new prophets, and a general renewal.[70] They say that all this will be of great benefit to the Christians, but first the world will be uprooted and cleansed, and then it will be replanted and rebuilt.

Be patient, for I have things to do.

Know this: that they have discovered the art of flying, the only art the world lacks, and they expect to discover a glass in which to see the hidden stars and a device by which to hear the music of the spheres.[71]

HOSPITALER. Oh, oh, oh! I like that. But Cancer is a feminine sign of Venus and of the moon. What good can it do?

GENOESE. They say that the feminine signs bring fecundity and foretell that a less vigorous power will have dominion over us. Thus it may be observed that our century has seen many women rulers—the Amazons between Nubia and Monopotapa[72] and, among the Europeans, Roxelana in Turkey, Bona in Poland, Mary in Hungary, Elizabeth in England, Catherine in France, Margaret in Flanders, Bianca in Tuscany, Mary in Scotland, Camilla in Rome, Isabella in Spain, the discoverer of the New World.[73] Moreover, the poet of this century began with women, saying:

Of ladies and of knights, of arms, of loves.[74]

And, besides, all the poets of our day are slanderers because of the influence of Mars; because of the influence of Venus and the moon they talk of pederasty and whoring.[75] Men are becoming effeminate and address each other as "Your Lordship";[76] in Africa where Can-

ci sono in Fez e Marocco li bordelli degli effeminati pu-
blici, e mille sporchezze.

Non però restò, per esser tropico segno Cancro ed
esaltazion di Giove e apogeo del Sole e di Marte trigono,
sì come per la Luna e Marte e Venere ha fatto la nova
invenzion del mondo e la stupenda maniera di girar
tutta la terra e l'imperio donnesco, e per Mercurio e
Marte e Giove le stampe e archibugi, di non far anche de
leggi gran mutamento. Chè nel Mondo Novo e in tutte
le marine d'Africa e Asia australi è entrato il cri-
stianesmo per Giove e Sole, e in Africa la legge del Se-
riffo per la Luna, e per Marte in Persia quella d'Alle,
renovata dal Sofì, con mutarsi imperio in tutte quelle
parti e in Tartaria. Ma in Germania, Francia e Inghil-
terra entrò l'eresia per esser esse a Marte e alla Luna in-
chinate; e Spagna per Giove e Italia per il Sole, a cui
sottostanno, per Sagittario e Leone, segni loro, restâro
nella bellezza della legge cristiana pura. E quante cose
saran più di mo inanzi, e quanto imparai da questi savi
circa la mutazion dell'asside de' pianeti e dell'eccentrici-
tà e solstizi ed equinozi e obliquitati, e poli variati e con-
fuse figure nello spazio immenso; e del simbolo c'hanno
le cose nostrali con quelle di fuori del mondo; e quanto
seque di mutamento dopo la congiunzion magna, e
l'eclissi, che sequeno dopo la congiunzion magna, in
Ariete e Libra, segni equinoziali, con la renovazione

cer reigns there are, besides the Amazons, houses of prostitution for effeminate males in both Fez and Morocco, and there are a thousand other filthy practices as well.

Just as Cancer, being a tropical sign, the exaltation of Jupiter,[77] the apogee of the sun and of trigonal Mars, brought about the new land discoveries, the wondrous method of circumnavigating the earth, and the dominance of women through the influence of the moon, Mars, and Venus; just as it brought about the invention of printing and of the harquebus through the influence of Mercury, Mars, and Jupiter, so did it bring about great changes in religion. In the New World and on the southern shores of Africa and Asia, Christianity was introduced through the influence of Jupiter and the sun, while in North Africa the law of the Sharīf was introduced through the influence of the moon;[78] in Persia, through the influence of Mars, the law of Allah was introduced, which was later restored by Sūfi when a new dynasty came to power in those parts and throughout Tartary.[79] But in Germany, France, and England heresy was introduced because these countries lean toward Mars and the moon, while Spain and Italy—the one being subject to Jupiter, the other to the sun, and both being influenced by Sagittarius and Leo, which are their signs—have remained under the happy dispensation of the pure Christian law. How many things I learned that are yet to happen! How much I learned from these wise people about changes in the apsides of planets, about eccentricities, solstices, equinoxes, obliquities, shifted poles, and confused figures out in the immensity of space! And how much I learned concerning the symbolic relation between things of earth and things out there, about the great changes that will be produced by the superior conjunction, and how the eclipses in Aries and Libra (equinoctial signs) that will follow upon the

dell'anomalie, faran cose stupende in confirmar il decreto della congiunzion magna e mutar tutto il mondo e rinovarlo!

Ma per tua fè, non mi trattener più, c'ho da fare. Sai come sto di pressa. Un'altra volta.

Questo si sappi, che essi tengon la libertà dell'arbitrio. E dicono che, se in quarant'ore di tormento un uomo non si lascia dire quel che si risolve tacere, manco le stelle, che inchinano con modi lontani, ponno sforzare. Ma perchè nel senso soavemente fan mutanza, chi segue più il senso che la raggione è soggetto a loro. Onde la costellazione che da Lutero cadavero cavò vapori infetti, da' Gesuini nostri che fûro al suo tempo cavò odorose esalazioni di virtù, e da Fernando Cortese che promulgò il cristianesmo in Messico nel medesimo tempo.

Ma di quanto è per sequire presto nel mondo io tel dirò un'altra fiata.

L'eresia è opera sensuale, come dice S. Paolo, e le stelle nelli sensuali inchinano a quella, nelli razionali alla vera legge santa della Prima Raggione, sempre laudanda. Amen.

OSPITALARIO. Aspetta, aspetta.

GENOVESE. Non posso, non posso.

great conjunction, together with the renewal of anomalies, will do stupendous things to confirm the decree of the great conjunction and transform the world completely and renew it.[80]

But I beg you, don't delay me any longer, for I have things to do. You know how pressed I am. Some other time.

Know this: that these people believe in the freedom of the will; and they say that if a man, after forty hours of torture, will not reveal what he has resolved to keep secret, then not even the stars working so far off can force him to do so.[81] But because the stars gently induce transformations in the senses, those who adhere to the senses more than to reason are subject to the stars.[82] Hence the constellation that drew infectious vapors from Luther's cadaver drew fragrant exhalations of virtue from the Jesuits[83] of that period and from Hernando Cortés, who established Christianity in Mexico at that same time.

But as to what is soon to happen in the world, I shall tell you about that some other time.

Heresy is a sensual act, as St. Paul says,[84] and the stars influence sensualists in that direction; rationalists they incline toward the true, holy law of the First Reason, ever to be praised. Amen.

HOSPITALER. Wait, Wait!

GENOESE. I can't, I can't.

Notes

1. A knight of Malta or, more fully, a knight of the Order of Hospitalers of St. John in Jerusalem.
2. Though some Renaissance maps of Asia situate Taprobana (or Taprobane) below the equator on the island of Sumatra—and this may be the location Campanella has in mind—earlier tradition identifies it with Ceylon. So too does Giovanni Botero, to whom Campanella is obviously indebted for a number of details. See his *Relationi universali* (1595; Venice, 1600), 2.2.24.
3. Since, as we shall learn, the Solarians honor the sun "as the symbol and visage of God" (p. 111), this alone may suffice to explain why Campanella chose to call his utopia the City of the Sun. Nevertheless, a number of sources may have suggested it to him, most notably Isaiah 19:18: "In that day there shall be five cities in the land of Egypt . . . one shall be called the city of the sun."
4. Speaking of Cambaia (in India), Botero mentions the famous city of "Campanel (which has seven encircling walls and is situated on a hill in the middle of a plain) . . ." (*Relationi*, 2.2.86).
5. Outworks with two faces forming a projecting salient angle.
6. The circles apparently represent the parallels and meridians.
7. In his annotations for the Italian text used for this translation, Firpo notes that in all the manuscripts of *The City of the Sun* the astrological symbol—a circle with a dot in the center—is substituted for the word *sun*, as though this was its form in the language of the Solarians. Hence the need to restate it "in our language."
8. Recalling the three persons of the Trinity.
9. Or *Fisico*. The only indication we have of his func-

tion appears on p. 59, where we learn that he determines when a child should be weaned.

10. That is, orally.

11. As is clear from what follows, the walls of the outermost circuit are not given over to illustrations, despite the inclusiveness of this statement.

12. It must be noted that in moving from the outer northern gate of the city to the temple at the center, Campanella identifies the outermost wall as the first. Having arrived at the temple and reversing direction, however, he also reverses the numerical order of the walls, calling the innermost first.

13. That is, through Pon, Sin, and Mor.

14. In refuting Plato's argument for the common ownership of property (*Republic* 462c), Aristotle remarks that such property receives the least attention since men have the greatest concern for what they own privately (*Politics* 1261b).

15. Firpo notes that Campanella was thirty-four years old when he wrote *The City of the Sun*.

16. In a letter of 1609 addressed to Pope Paul V, Campanella affirmed that he could teach all the arts and sciences in just one year to any person capable of learning. There too he had in mind the invaluable "visual aids" with which the City of the Sun is furnished.

17. That is, a knowledge they could acquire by studying the illustrations and specimens exhibited on the city walls.

18. That is, in the vernal and autumnal equinoxes and in the summer and winter solstices.

19. Thus, according to Campanella, a favorable hour for sexual coupling occurs when the following celestial conditions obtain: (1) when Mercury and Venus appear on the horizon before the sun (and are therefore said to be oriental to it); (2) when both these planets are in a benefic house, i.e., any one of the twelve astrological divisions of the celestial

sphere (each extending 30°) from which they exert a strong benefic influence; (3) when Jupiter, Saturn, and Mars are each favorably positioned (and therefore in benefic aspect) relative to Mercury and Venus, the sun and the moon. This last condition is met when the last mentioned four bodies are each either 30°, 60°, or 120° from both Mercury and Venus. The term *apheta* (or *dator vita* or *hylec* or *prorogator*) is assigned to the celestial body or portion of the zodiac that starts the subject of the horoscope on his career and determines the length of his life.

20. In other words, they seek a time when Virgo, the sixth zodiacal sign, is just about to rise above the eastern horizon (i.e., is in the ascendant) and when neither Saturn nor Mars is in any of the four astrological houses (the angles) located at the cardinal points of the compass. When two celestial bodies are in opposition, they are 180° apart or diametrically opposite one another; when they are in quadrature, they are 90° apart or at right angles to one another.

21. Astrologers usually regard Saturn and Mars as malefic, especially with regard to generation, the one because it is believed cold, the other because it is believed dry. A planet is called the ruler when it is in the sign of the zodiac assigned to it as its house. See also n. 19 above.

22. See *Republic* 460a.

23. As Firpo notes, more recent and reliable estimates put the population of Naples close to two hundred thousand near the end of the sixteenth century.

24. For the same reason More's Utopians found six hours each day more than enough.

25. Campanella is referring to the game of *ruzzola*, in which the object was to roll a wooden disk as far as possible down an inclined path with one swing of the arm.

26. In his fifth epistle St. Clement approves the com-

munal ownership of all things including women (Migne, *Patrologia Latina* 130.57). Gratian quotes the relevant passage of this epistle in his *Decretum* (2.12.qu.1) and offers a correction, citing Tertullian's *Apologeticus adversus gentes pro Christianis* (Migne, *Patrologia Latina* 1.472) as his authority. There Tertullian writes: "With us everything is in common except wives."

27. In his *Lives of Eminent Philosophers* (2.5.26), Diogenes Laertius mentions some writers who claimed that Socrates had two wives at the same time, this having been permitted by an Athenian law intended to increase the population. After his beloved Marcia had borne him several children, Cato the Younger yielded to the entreaties of his friend Hortensius and divorced her so that Hortensius himself might marry her and beget children by her. Years later, when Marcia had become a widow, Cato remarried her. Plato is cited here for the views expressed in his *Republic*.

28. Firpo notes that this statement first appeared in Campanella's 1611 revision. It reflects his conviction that there is no inconsistency or contradiction between right reason and revealed religion, the latter being no more than an extension of the former. Thomas More likewise believed that his Utopians would embrace Christianity as soon as it was revealed to them.

29. Campanella associates the Brahmans with the Pythagoreans because of their common belief in metempsychosis, or the transmigration of souls.

30. In the *Metamorphoses* (12.71–145) Ovid tells how Cygnus, though his father Neptune had made him invulnerable, was slain by Achilles, who, being unable to wound him with spear or sword, strangled him with the thongs of his own helmet. Immediately Cygnus then became a swan.

31. It is not entirely clear how this invention of Cam-

panella's was to be constructed. Apparently, each stirrup was to consist of a rather large metal ring or shallow cylinder bounding an equilateral triangle composed of three metal braces. The strap connecting the stirrup to the saddle was to be buckled loosely around both the ring or cylinder and the triangle, while the reins, after being crossed at the saddle, were to be buckled only to the ring or cylinder. Thus, by exerting pressure with his foot on any side of the triangle, the rider could wind or unwind the reins according to the direction he wanted his horse to take.

32. Though he detested Machiavelli's political views, Campanella seems here to be echoing the Florentine's oft-repeated advice that any injuries a victor must inflict upon his vanquished foe should be inflicted at one stroke if possible (see especially *The Prince*, chapter 8).

33. A title no doubt suggested by Virgil's *Georgics*, just as the *Buccolica* named below was suggested by his *Bucolics*.

34. See Genesis 30:25–43. The breeding method mentioned here recalls how Jacob got Laban's goats to bear spotted and speckled kids and his sheep to bear dark-colored lambs. The goats were encouraged to mate while they faced rods from which he had whittled off strips of bark, and the sheep while they faced the dark-colored goats. His magic, in other words, like Campanella's, involved visual suggestion.

35. That is, in domestic animals slaughtered for consumption before maturity.

36. The fixed signs are Leo, Scorpio, Aquarius, and Taurus, each 90° from the next and each representing one of the four elements (fire, water, air, and earth respectively). They are believed to be particularly powerful and, taken together, represent a balance of opposing forces. In general Campa-

nella's meaning seems to be this: before founding
their city, the Solarians, employing electional as-
trology, tried to find a time for doing so that would
be auspicious to its "dominion, stability and great-
ness." Such a time, they discovered, would have
the named celestial bodies disposed to one another
as Campanella indicates: with the fixed signs
"set . . . at the four corners of the world" and with
the sun, preceded by Jupiter, on the point of rising
(i.e., in the ascendant) above the eastern horizon in
the sign of Leo, etc. Of the three astrological houses
mentioned (the ninth, fourth, and tenth), the first
was associated with foundations, religion, and
learning, the second with cities in general, and the
third with rulers. Hence all are particularly relevant
to the aims the Solarians had in mind. It should be
added, however, that if they delayed founding their
city until all the mentioned celestial conditions
were met, they must have waited a very long time.
I owe to Professor Wayne Shumaker the suggestion
that Campanella may have been thinking of an ar-
millary sphere upon which the Solarians simply ar-
ranged the celestial bodies in the manner they
judged propitious to the city. Alternatively, they
could have so arranged the "celestial globe" men-
tioned as resting on the altar of their temple (p. 31).
For other astrological terms that appear in this pas-
sage, see nn. 19 and 20 above.

37. Fortune, more commonly called the Lot of Fortune
or the Part of Fortune, is a point on the celestial
sphere which the astrologer locates by a computa-
tion based on the position of the sun, the moon, and
the ascendant. The Head of Medusa, otherwise
called the Demon Star or Algol, is the variable star
Beta in the constellation Perseus.

38. Astrology locates four triplicities in the zodiac,
each one representing one of the four elements and
composed of three zodiacal signs that form an equi-

lateral triangle. Here Campanella seems to be referring to the third or airy triplicity, associated with intellect and formed by Gemini, Libra, and Aquarius, which Mercury is said to rule by night; but his reference to the latter's apsis—either extremity of its elliptical orbit—is puzzling in this context, though Mercury in fact has the second most elliptical orbit in the solar system. Also puzzling is Campanella's use of *aspect* and *conjunction* in reference to a planet (Mercury) and a zodiacal sign (Virgo), rather than to two planets as is invariably the case. A conjunction occurs when two planets, as seen by an observer on earth, are no more than about 8° apart. It is one of the six aspects generally recognized by astrologers, the others being opposition, quadrature, sestile, semisestile, and trigonal, when two planets are respectively either 180°, 90°, 60°, or 120° apart. Conjunctions can produce both benefic and malefic results, very strong ones in either case. The god Mercury, associated with trade and thievery, and the planet named for him were considered untrustworthy. The latter was believed to take on the color of any other planet in aspect with it. Jove, or Jupiter, on the other hand, was regarded as the planet that could do no evil.

39. Epilepsy, called *morbus sacer* by the Romans.
40. That is, Power, Wisdom, and Love.
41. Apparently Sun has no subordinate officials except Pon, Sin, and Mor assigned to him; otherwise the number thirteen would be incorrect.
42. The Metaphysician may reduce the sentence but cannot alter the verdict.
43. Sacks containing gunpowder would be attached to the condemned man's body and set afire, killing him almost instantly.
44. Initiated shortly before 1540, probably in Milan, this service consisted of a round of prayer before the exposed Blessed Sacrament lasting forty hours

135

and terminating at one church just as it began at another, thus continuing the year around.

45. See n. 18 above.

46. As Firpo notes, Campanella may be alluding here to the worship of saints and of holy relics.

47. It should be recalled that the altar is exposed to the sky. See p. 31.

48. For Aaron's priestly robes, see Exodus 38.

49. The tropical year ends about twenty minutes sooner than the sidereal year. The former is the measure of time the sun requires to return to the same position with respect to the equinoctial points; the latter is the measure of time it requires to return to the same position with respect to the fixed stars.

50. The moon's path through the zodiac inclines to the ecliptic (the sun's path) by about 5°. The two points at which it crosses the ecliptic were called the Dragon's Head and the Dragon's Tail and are now commonly called the lunar nodes. These move slowly along the ecliptic from east to west, completing their cycle in about nineteen years.

51. Aristarchus of Samos (early third century B.C.) and his predecessor Philolaus (fifth century B.C.) both believed in the earth's rotation around the sun.

52. By this Campanella means that both Ptolemy and Copernicus offer mere mathematical abstractions, hypotheses and not realities, to account for what we see in the heavens, and these abstractions are to the truth as play money is to gold.

53. "Immediately after the tribulation of these days shall the sun be darkened, and the moon shall not give her light, and the stars shall fall from heaven, and the powers of the heavens shall be shaken" (Matthew 24:29; see also Mark 13:24–25 and Luke 21:25).

54. Among numerous biblical references to the world's end coming as a thief in the night, see 2 Peter 3:10: "But the day of the Lord will come as a thief in the

night, in which the heavens shall pass away with a great noise."

55. This is worship due lawfully only to God, as distinguished from *dulia*, worship of saints and angels, and from *hyperdulia*, worship of the Virgin Mary.

56. It will be recalled that in substituting his simpler heliocentric system for Ptolemy's geocentric one, Copernicus reduced but did not abandon the use of epicycles and eccentrics to explain celestial movements. The astronomical theories summarily and obscurely presented in this and in the following paragraphs reflect Campanella's own views as adopted from Telesio. See Introduction, pp. 5–6.

57. In other words, the planets (including the moon) act in this way because of the attraction of solar heat and the repulsion of terrestrial cold. See also n. 38 above.

58. But apparently Campanella means planets, not stars.

59. Firpo notes that at this point in the original manuscript Campanella supplied the marginal annotation "somewhat obscure; but it contains the truth, though it seems a lie." In a later manuscript this was replaced by the statement "on this matter much is said in our *Astronomia*," a work Campanella began in 1603. It was seized by the authorities in 1611, when the author was in prison, and was later lost.

60. Since, according to Genesis 1:2, there were trees bearing fruit on the third day.

61. Or, stated differently, sin can have no efficient cause.

62. Any act arising from impotence or ignorance is not a sin. Only the will, which precedes both power and wisdom, can sin.

63. *The Statesman*, 269a.

64. Taking any point within an elliptical or eccentric orbit, the apsides would be the two points of the orbit which are respectively farthest from it (apo-

gee) or nearest to it (perigree). In saying that ". . . changes in the apsides . . . every thousand six hundred years produce great changes in the world," Campanella was thinking no doubt of the year 1600, which he had predicted would see great political upheavals. His conviction that this would be a fateful year inspired him in 1599 to lead or at least take part in an insurrection against the Spaniards in his native Calabria, which would result in nearly thirty years of captivity for him. See Introduction, pp. 8 ff.

65. A superior or great conjunction involves three or more planets (see n. 38 above). Irregularities in planetary motions are called anomalies.

66. This is a somewhat veiled denial of the doctrine of original sin.

67. Or, as stated affirmatively: "And as ye would that men should do to you, do ye also to them likewise" (Luke 6:31).

68. Despite the solecism ("present century" versus "the whole world"), Campanella's point is clear. The correct comparison would be between the "present century" and the "preceding four thousand years."

69. The fourth triplicity (Cancer, Scorpio, Pisces) is the watery; the first, mentioned in the next sentence, is the fiery (Aries, Leo, Sagittarius). But see also n. 38 above.

70. This is a reference to the bright star that appeared in the constellation Cassiopeia in 1572, upon which Tycho Brahe wrote *De nova stella* in the following year. He wrote of it again in his *Astronomiae instauratae progymnasmata* (published by Kepler in 1602). According to Firpo this work did not become known to Campanella until February 1611. The reference, therefore, is lacking in the earliest manuscripts of *The City of the Sun*.

71. As an astronomical instrument the telescope at-

tracted little attention until 1609, when Galileo constructed one and used it for the important observations he reported in the *Sidereus nuncius* in the following year. Campanella read it in the same year and shortly after wrote an enthusiastic letter to the author. The reference to a "glass" here, as Firpo notes, had therefore to be added to the manuscript in 1611 or later.

72. Or, more correctly, Monomopotapa; though Botero, who is Campanella's source here again, also wrote Monopotapa. See his *Relationi* (1.3.172), where this is given as the name of a prince whose best warriors were women who conducted themselves much as the ancient Amazons did. The territory over which Monopotapa ruled corresponds roughly with that of present day Tanzania and northern Mozambique.

73. The first eight ladies mentioned here are, in order: Roxelana, favorite of Suleyman the Magnificent and mother of Selim II; Bona Sforza, wife of Sigismund I of Poland; Mary of Hapsburg, wife of Louis II of Hungary; Elizabeth I of England; Catherine de' Medici, wife of Henry II of France; Margaret of Austria, mother of Alessandro Farnese, Duke of Parma and for some years Regent of Flanders; Bianca Capello, mistress and later wife of Francesco I, Grand Duke of Tuscany; and Mary Queen of Scots. The identity of the next named lady is obscure. Firpo believes that she was Camilla Peretti, the much beloved sister of Pope Sixtus V, but there is little evidence that she exercised political or ecclesiastical power or was a ruler in any sense. Isabella, Queen of Aragon and Castile, is the last mentioned, though, unlike all the others, she really belongs to the fifteenth rather than to the sixteenth century since she died in 1504.

74. The poet referred to is Ludovico Ariosto, author of *Orlando Furioso*, the first line of which is quoted.

75. Astrologers generally regard Mars as the most malefic planet of all; Venus, of course, is associated with sensuality, as the moon is with changeability.

76. The gender of the Italian equivalent—*vossignoria*— is feminine.

77. A planet is most potent when it is in exaltation and least potent when it is in dejection. For Jupiter these conditions obtain when it is respectively in Cancer and Capricorn. Trigon is usually a synonym for triplicity. See n. 38 above.

78. The Sadī Sharīf dynasty, claiming descent from Fatima, Muhammad's sister, ruled Morocco from 1548 to 1659.

79. Sūfi, as Firpo notes, was the name loosely used in the West to designate the ruler of Persia. It is not to be confused with Sufism, a form of Islamic mysticism. Campanella is referring to the Safavid dynasty that ruled from 1502 to 1736.

80. See nn. 64 and 65 above.

81. As proof that man has free will, here Campanella offers his own experience, the strength with which he held out against his torturers when in 1601 he was subjected to *la veglia*. See Introduction, p. 11.

82. "The majority of men follow their passions, which are movements of the sensitive appetite, in which movements heavenly bodies can cooperate, but few are sufficiently wise to resist these passions. Consequently, astrologers are able to foretell the truth in the majority of cases, especially in a general way. But not in particular cases, for nothing prevents man's resisting his passions by his free will" (St. Thomas Aquinas, *Summa theologica* 1.115.4).

83. Campanella's word here is *Gesuini*, not *Gesuiti*, which is the more correct form if he means Jesuits. However, it is at least possible, as Professor Fredi Chiappelli has suggested to me, that Campanella is instead referring to the *Gesuati*, also called *Gesuatini*, members of a humble religious order, dedicated to prayer and works of charity, that was

founded by Giovanni Colombini in 1360 and dissolved by Clement IX in 1668.

84. "Now the works of the flesh are manifest, which are these; Adultery, fornication, uncleanness, lasciviousness, idolatry, witchcraft, hatred, variance, emulation, wrath, strife, seditions, heresies" (Galatians 5:19–20).

Selected Bibliography

Amabile, Luigi. *Fra Tommaso Campanella: La sua congiura, i suoi processi e la sua pazzia*. 3 vols. Napoli: 1882.

————. *Fra Tommaso Campanella nei castelli di Napoli, in Roma ed in Parigi*. 2 vols. Napoli: 1887.

Amerio, Romano et al. *Campanella e Vico*. Padova: 1969.

————. *Il sistema teologico di Tommaso Campanella*. Milano–Napoli: 1972.

Badaloni, Nicola. *Tommaso Campanella*. Milano: 1965.

Blanchet, Leon. *Campanella*. Paris: 1920.

Bonansea, Bernardino M. *Tommaso Campanella: Renaissance Pioneer of Modern Thought*. Washington, D.C.: 1969.

Di Napoli, Giovanni. *Tommaso Campanella, filosofo della restaurazione cattolica*. Padova: 1947.

Eurich, Nell. *Science in Utopias*. Cambridge, Mass.: 1967.

Firpo, Luigi. *Bibliografia degli scritti di Tommaso Campanella*. Torino: 1940.

————. *Scritti scelti di Giordano Bruno e Tommaso Campanella*. Torino: 1949.

————. *Tutte le opere di Tommaso Campanella*. Vol. 1. Milano: 1954.

Garin, Eugenio. *La cultura filosofica del Rinascimento italiano*. Firenze: 1961.

————. *Italian Humanism*. Translated by Peter Munz. Oxford: 1966.

Gentile, Giovanni. *Studi sul Rinascimento*. Firenze: 1923.

————. *Il pensiero italiano del Rinascimento*. Firenze: 1940.

Grillo, Francesco. *Tommaso Gampanella in America: A Critical Bibliography and a Profile*. New York: 1954.

————. *Tommaso Campanella in America: A Supplement to the Critical Bibliography*. New York: 1957.

Kelly-Gadol, Joan. "Tommaso Campanella: The Agony of Political Theory in the Counter-Reformation." In *Philosophy and Humanism: Renaissance Essays in Honor of Paul Oskar Kristeller*, edited by Edward P. Mahoney, pp. 164–89. Leiden: 1976.

143

McColley, Grant, trans. and ed. *The Defense of Galileo of Tommaso Campanella*. Northampton, Mass.: 1937.

Morley, Henry, ed. *Ideal Commonwealths*. London: 1893. Reprint. Port Washington, N.Y.: 1968.

Treves, Paolo. *La filosofia politica di Tommaso Campanella*. Bari: 1930.

Walker, D. P. *Spiritual and Demonic Magic from Ficino to Campanella*. London: 1958.

Designer: Wolfgang Lederer
Compositor: G & S Typesetters, Inc.
Printer: Thomson-Shore, Inc.
Binder: John H. Dekker & Sons, Inc.
Text: VIP Bembo
Display: VIP Bembo
Cloth: Joanna Arrestox B 34000
Paper: 50 lb P & S offset B-32